THE BELIEFS I NEVER CHOSE

How Inherited Mindsets Shape Identity,

Self-Talk, and the Life We Live

Robin DeFleice

ISBN: 979-8-9947633-2-2

Published by Quiet Authority Press

Book Cover by Ayesha Zaheer

ACKNOWLEDGMENTS

This book is the result of a journey I never planned but desperately needed.

It would not exist without the people, teachers, and experiences that challenged me, guided me, and ultimately freed me.

To my mother, who taught me obedience before I learned questioning, I now understand that you were teaching me what you were taught. You gave me what you had. And while I've had to examine and release some of what was handed down, I honor the strength, resilience, and survival instincts you passed on. You did the best you could with what you knew.

To my grandfather, whose words—"The white man ain't gonna never let you have anything"—stayed with me for decades. I understand now that you were speaking from experience, from pain, from the reality you lived. While I've chosen to release that belief, I honor the struggle you endured and the truth you knew. Your experience was real. But it doesn't have to be my destiny.

To the teachers whose voices I carried for too long—the ones who told me to stay quiet, stay small, stay in line—I release you with gratitude. You taught me what conformity looked like. And in recognizing it, I learned to choose something different.

To Dr. Bruce Lipton, Dr. Joe Dispenza, Gregg Braden, and Dr. Caroline Leaf—your research gave me the scientific language for what I had been experiencing spiritually. You showed me that belief shapes biology, that thought creates reality, and that the mind can be reprogrammed. Your work validated my questions and gave me tools to create real change. Thank you for bridging science and spirituality in a way that made transformation tangible.

To Neville Goddard and Joseph Murphy—though I never met you, your teachings reached me through books and recordings that felt like they were written specifically for me. You taught me that imagination creates reality, that feeling is the secret, and that the "I Am" is the most powerful statement I can make. Your words became my foundation.

To Joyce Meyer—I heard you teach Romans 12:2 countless times: "Be transformed by the renewing of your mind." For years, I didn't fully understand it. But when I did, it became the key that unlocked everything. Thank you for making biblical truth accessible and practical.

To Napoleon Hill—Think and Grow Rich didn't just teach me about money. It taught me about mindset, belief, and the power of thought. Your work planted seeds that took years to grow, but when they did, they changed my life.

To Edgar Cayce—your writings introduced me to meditation and the idea that wisdom exists within. You opened a door I didn't know existed, and I've been walking through it ever since.

To the HeartMath Institute—your research on heart-brain coherence gave me a practice that literally changed my body, my mind, and my life. The Quick Coherence® Technique became my daily anchor. Thank you for proving that the heart is not just a pump—it's a center of intelligence.

To the community at Keller Williams—you welcomed me when I took the biggest risk of my life. You believed in me before I fully believed in myself. You gave me a space to become the top real estate agent I declared I would be. Thank you for being part of my transformation.

To the food bank where I volunteer—serving others has been one of the most profound practices of abundance. In giving, I reinforce the belief that there is enough. That I have enough. That I am enough. Thank you for allowing me to be part of something bigger than myself.

To the clients I served as a case manager—you taught me more than I ever taught you. I saw systems fail you. I saw the cost of blind trust in institutions. I saw how people can be trapped in cycles not of their making. Your experiences woke me up. They made me question. And in questioning, I found my path to freedom. Thank you.

To my friend who still believes "everything breaks down when you get old"—I don't judge you. I understand you. And I'm grateful that your belief helped me see my own. In distancing myself from your mindset, I protected my growth. That was painful, but necessary. I wish you peace.

To the woman at the doctor's office who said, "I trust my doctor"—I don't know if you'll ever read this, but your words haunted me. They showed me what surrender looks like. And they reminded me why this work matters. I hope one day you discover that your body has wisdom too.

To everyone who questioned my questions, who got angry when I examined faith, who feared when I left the herd, who doubted when I quit my job with no backup plan, thank you. Your resistance showed me how deeply programming runs. It reminded me why this work is so hard, and why it's so necessary. I don't resent you. I understand you. Because I was you.

To the parts of myself I had to release—the identity of "the strong one who doesn't need help," the belief that "I'm not good enough," the fear that "it won't last" I honor you for protecting me when I needed protection. But you don't serve me anymore. I release you with gratitude and love.

To the reader holding this book—if you've made it this far, you're already doing the work. You're already questioning. You're already waking up. That takes courage. I see you. And I'm honored to walk this path with you.

And finally, to the voice within me that never stopped asking "why"—even when I was told not to question, even when it was easier to conform, even when doubt felt like betrayal—thank you for never giving up. You knew there was more. You knew I was capable of more. You knew the beliefs I carried were not the whole truth.

You were right.

This book is proof that questioning leads to freedom.

And freedom leads to life.

With deep gratitude and love,

Robin DeFleice

Table of Contents

PART I: AWAKENING

CHAPTER 1

The Voice That Isn't Yours

I spent most of my life living according to beliefs I never chose.

They came from my mother, my family, my culture, my faith, my community. They were delivered as commands, repeated as truth, and reinforced through tone, silence, and consequence. I didn't question them because I didn't know I could. I didn't examine them because I didn't realize they were just beliefs—not facts.

For years, I thought the voice in my head was my own.

The one that said I wasn't good enough to become what I dreamed of being, not someone from where I came from. It warned me to stay small because, as my mother would say, *"I don't want you to get hurt by this world."* That voice that told me life was full of limits, and I should be grateful for what I had. The one that whispered, *"Who do you think you are? You don't have what it takes."*

But that voice didn't originate with me. It was learned. Inherited. Programmed into my subconscious as a child. The strange part was, I always felt something was off. I just didn't know what it was—but it was running my life.

This book is about waking up to that reality—and doing something about it.

It's about recognizing that the beliefs handed down to us, no matter how well-intentioned, are not always right. That some beliefs are like pacifiers, meant to soothe fear or maintain order. That other beliefs are outright lies, repeated so often they feel like wisdom. And that the most dangerous beliefs are the ones we never dare question.

This is not a book about rejecting your past or dishonoring those who raised you. This is a book about reclaiming authority over your own mind. About examining what you were taught, keeping the beliefs that serve you, and releasing what limits you. About understanding that you are not required to carry beliefs that were true for someone else but not true for you.

The Bible says it clearly in Romans 12:2: *"Do not be conformed to this world but be transformed by the renewing of your mind."*

Transformation happens through renewal. Not through more information—but through examining and changing what you believe.

Joyce Meyer has shared this verse for decades, reminding us that the mind is where transformation begins. Not in trying harder. Not in performing better. But in renewing—reprogramming—what was inadvertently placed there.

This is the work of this book.

I wrote this book because I lived it.

I lived with unexamined beliefs about money, food, my body, success, God, systems, and my own worthiness. I lived in the gap between what I was told and what I actually thought. I performed beliefs I didn't hold. I stayed silent when I had questions. I abandoned myself to keep the peace.

And it cost me. I remember when I was in school, we had the option to choose a higher education path or the labor force path. The teacher asked what I wanted to be when I grew up, and I told him I wanted to be a nurse. I remember this tall, white, lanky guy leaning in and saying, *"You're not college material."* I was 10 years old at the time. Fifty-eight years later, I still remember it as if it were yesterday. Things like this added to the *you're not good enough* programming.

It cost me years of living small. Years of second-guessing myself. Years of staying in spaces—jobs, relationships, mindsets—that were never designed for my growth. Years of believing the life I wanted wasn't meant for people like me.

But then I started questioning.

And questioning changed everything.

I questioned my faith. I questioned authority. I questioned the systems I had been taught to trust. I questioned the beliefs I had about money, health, success, and myself. And what I discovered was this: most of what I believed wasn't based on my own experience, discernment, or truth. It was based on inherited programming.

Programming, I learned, can be rewritten.

This book is the map of that journey—from unconscious living to conscious choice. From inherited beliefs to examined truth. From the voice that was never mine to the voice I chose for myself.

If you've ever felt like something is off—like the beliefs, you were given don't quite fit the person you're becoming—this book is for you.

If you've ever questioned something you were taught and felt guilty for doubting—this book is for you.

If you've ever wondered why life feels so heavy, so limited, so misaligned—this book is for you.

The beliefs you never chose are not permanent.
The voice in your head is not the final authority.
And the life you were told wasn't possible for you?
It's waiting on the other side of questioning.

CHAPTER 2

The Beliefs I Never Chose

Some of the strongest beliefs in my life were running on autopilot.

They were handed down to me as a child—through family, culture, faith, survival, and circumstance. I accepted them as truth because I had no reason to question them. I didn't examine them. I didn't challenge them. I simply lived by them.

Those beliefs became the lens through which I saw the world. They shaped how I understood love, success, failure, God, safety, and myself. My decisions were built on them. My reactions were guided by them. I didn't realize it at the time, but I was living inside a system of beliefs I never consciously chose.

The Ants in the Jar

I remember hearing a story that made me think years later about how being trapped physically and mentally are two completely different things.

A boy put ants in a jar. Naturally, the ants tried to escape—climbing to the top of the jar to get out. So, the boy decided to put a cap on the jar. The ants kept trying for a while, but eventually, they stopped. They accepted the cap as their reality. They gave up.

Then the boy removed the cap, and to his surprise, none of the ants tried to escape.

The jar was open. Freedom was available. But the ants didn't leave. They had grown so accustomed to the limitation that even when it was removed, they stayed trapped. Not because they had to—but because they believed they had to.

This is what happens with inherited beliefs.

The cap gets internalized.

And even when circumstances change, even when the limitation is no longer real, we remain trapped inside beliefs that no longer serve us. We stay small in a jar that no longer has a lid.

Growing up, I dared not question authority, especially my mother.

My mother was clear: do not question me. Do not talk back. Do not ask why.

Obedience was valued over understanding. Silence was safer than curiosity. Respect meant compliance, not conversation. Beliefs were handed down without explanation—delivered as instruction, as law, as something not to be examined but accepted.

That lesson didn't stay in childhood. It followed me into adulthood.

If you are taught early that questioning authority is wrong, you don't just stop questioning people, you stop questioning ideas.

Some beliefs are not lies, but they are not truth either. They are placeholders—ideas meant to ease worry, endure order, or help people survive difficult circumstances. Placeholders are often put in place to cover confusion and inherited programming. Because if you were programmed, so were your parents and grandparents. It was not done intentionally; it is how humans are conditioned for life. These beliefs can calm us when we are young, but they can also keep us from developing fully.

Other beliefs are outright lies. Lies dressed as wisdom. Lies repeated so often they feel familiar. Lies that sound like protection but quietly limit our growth.

The real danger isn't believing a lie. The danger is never questioning it.

As I reflect on the beliefs that were handed down without explanation, I recall being told that men are better at math, that women are better at nurturing. We were even told that something was wrong with you if you were left-handed. I remember how hard my mother and her teachers tried to make my sister become right-handed. It didn't work, but the programming and beliefs she was left with was, something is wrong with me.

Belief shapes perception. Perception guides decisions.

But what happens when the belief is not true?

Then perception is off. Decisions are warped. And life—built on those decisions—begins to feel confusing, heavy, and misaligned.

This is where doubt enters.

Doubt is not the enemy. Doubt is the invitation. Confusion is not failure. Confusion is evidence that something inside you is waking up.

Beliefs can be examined. Beliefs can be refined. Beliefs can be replaced.

Before I could change the voice in my head, before I could live intentionally instead of reactively, I had to examine what I had been taught to believe.

Truth is not always what we were given. Sometimes truth is what remains after we dare to ask questions.

CHAPTER 3

Who Taught Me What to Believe

Beliefs don't appear out of nowhere.

They are taught, modeled, repeated, and reinforced. According to Bruce Lipton, *"A child below 7 has a lower vibration than consciousness. It's called theta brainwaves. Theta is imagination... Theta is hypnosis. You just watch. You watch your parents, you watch your siblings, and your community."* In those early years, there are few real choices—you absorb whatever surrounds you.

Family was my first classroom. Not through lectures, but through tone, rules, reactions, and silence. I learned what was rewarded and what was punished. What questions were welcome—and which ones were not.

Culture reinforced what family introduced. Growing up, I was often confused about where I actually belonged. My grandmother was, in today's terms, considered very bougie, while my mother was in many ways the opposite. Grannie, as we called her, was an Eastern Star and a non-practicing Methodist. My mother was uneducated, dysfunctional, and newly Catholic.

As a Black woman, many beliefs were rooted in survival. Strength over softness. Endurance over rest. Responsibility over personal freedom. These beliefs did not come from malice. They came from experience. From generations navigating systems that were not designed to protect them. When I think about my early years and the confusion I carried, it is no wonder I had to do this work of reprogramming.

I remember my mother saying this when I wanted to get my hair braided —a common transition for Black girls moving away from the Afro style: *"Why you need to braid your hair... everybody know you Black."* What made her say that? That statement stayed with me, but the reason behind it mattered even more than the words themselves.

Faith added another layer.

As I stated before, my mother was raised in a non-practicing Methodist/Baptist environment, yet somehow my siblings and I were raised Catholic. Later in life, it occurred to me that God had been labeled as Him. I wondered, why not Her? Then I wondered how God could be labeled at all. But at the time, I accepted it as truth.

It's curious—people often become angry when faith is questioned. Not because the question is wrong, but because belief is foundational. When belief holds up someone's entire worldview, doubt can feel like collapse.

But questioning faith is not losing faith. It is deepening it.

Faith that cannot be questioned is fragile. Faith that allows inquiry becomes personal, expansive, and honest.

Society reinforces this pattern of unquestioned authority.

We are taught not to question doctors, teachers, police, or experts. Questioning is labeled disrespect. Curiosity is treated as defiance. Those who question are often seen as troublemakers or outsiders.

I remember asking the pastor why we kept studying the same scriptures over and over, but I was shut down and was never given a reason why we never studied the whole book.

Growing up, we believed the clergy were right, doctors were right, and even when they weren't, we believed they had our best interests at heart.

We put our faith in the news. Books. Newspapers. Advertisements. Medical studies.

Belief was blind.

I once spoke with a woman who had been diagnosed with diabetes and had been with the same doctor since childhood. I told her I had reversed my diabetes through diet. She told me she believed it could be reversed, but her doctor didn't believe it could be reversed, so he continued prescribing medication.

Her final statement was simple: *"I trust my doctor."*

What struck me wasn't her trust—it was her surrender.

This is how self-abandonment begins. Quietly. When we stop trusting our observations because authority feels safer. When credentials outweigh lived experience. When silence feels easier than questioning.

Questioning authority is not rebellion. It is responsibility.

The Pattern Everywhere: From Santa to Science

This pattern of unquestioned belief isn't limited to family and faith. It's woven throughout our entire culture.

The Lies We're Taught to Accept

As children, our first lesson in mass deception often comes gift-wrapped: Santa Claus. The Easter Bunny. The Tooth Fairy. Every adult in our lives—parents, grandparents, teachers—participates in the same coordinated lie. And when we finally learn the truth, we're told it was done out of fun.

This teaches us early:

• Authority figures lie to you with good intentions

• Everyone can agree on something false

• Questioning the consensus makes you the problem

• You'll be mocked for believing what you were taught to believe

The Feuds We Inherit

Some beliefs become generational warfare. The Hatfield-McCoy feud lasted decades. Most participants had no idea what started it—something about a stolen pig, a murdered brother, or an unpaid debt. The details didn't matter. What mattered was that you were born into an enemy.

They killed for beliefs they never questioned. They died for hatred they inherited.

How many of us carry smaller versions of this? Family grudges. Cultural animosities. Political allegiances. Ask yourself: Did I choose this position, or did I inherit it?

The Science That Isn't Science

Then there's the authority of science and medicine—which we're taught never to question.

Ten thousand steps a day. Everyone knows this is the goal for good health. Doctors recommend it. Fitness trackers measure it. Health articles repeat it.

But it didn't come from research. It came from a 1960s marketing campaign for a Japanese pedometer called *Manpo-kei*—which translates to *10,000 steps meter*. A company picked a round number that sounded good, and we've been repeating it as fact ever since.

This is just one example. The food pyramid—influenced by industry interests as much as nutrition guidance. Studies showing sugar was safe— funded by the sugar industry, which paid researchers to shift blame toward fat. Pharmaceutical studies funded by the very companies selling the drugs.

I'm not saying all science is corrupt. I'm saying we stopped questioning.

We believed because someone in authority said it. We didn't ask: Who funded this study? Who benefits from this belief? What's the evidence?

The Cost of Not Questioning

What all these examples have in common is this: beliefs presented as facts, accepted without examination, and passed down as truth.

And the cost? We spend our lives living according to information we never verified, from sources we never questioned, serving interests we never considered.

Questioning isn't revolt. It's being responsible.

When we stop questioning, we stop participating in our own lives.

Understanding where our beliefs came from gives us the power to decide which ones still belong to us.

CHAPTER 4

When Belief Becomes the Voice in Your Head

Beliefs don't stay outside of us.

Once repeated often enough, they move in. What began as someone else's rule, warning, or worldview eventually becomes our internal narrator. This is how belief turns into mindset—and mindset becomes self-talk.

By the time we reach adulthood, no one has to tell us what to believe out loud anymore. We do it ourselves.

The voice in your head did not originate there. It was learned.

If you were taught not to question, your inner voice begins questioning you instead.

"Don't ask." "Don't risk it." "Be grateful." "Who do you think you are?"

Mindset is not just how we think—it is what we assume is possible, allowed, or safe.

Unexamined belief hardens into mental habit.

For a long time, I believed struggle was normal, ease was suspicious, rest had to be earned, and success required sacrifice. These weren't conscious choices. They were conclusions formed through repetition.

Self-talk becomes the enforcement mechanism.

This is why changing self-talk without examining belief rarely works.

You cannot silence a voice that believes it is protecting you. You have to understand what it is protecting—and why.

Reversing negative self-talk does not begin with positivity. It begins with discernment.

Instead of asking, *"Why am I so negative?"* ask: What belief is this thought serving, and where did it come from?

Money beliefs. Food beliefs. Authority beliefs. Body beliefs. Each one carries a story.

When I began tracing these beliefs, I saw how deeply they were tied to systems. I was told money doesn't grow on trees. That we couldn't afford this or that. Scarcity was taught without strategy.

I was told to eat everything on my plate because the folks in Africa were starving—as if my obedience could solve suffering on another continent. Nourishment was replaced with guilt.

This is where unquestioned beliefs become dangerous.

By adulthood, I carried extra weight. And the voice in my head wasn't kind about it.

"You have no self-control." "Why can't you just stop eating?" "You're weak."

But the real problem wasn't willpower. It was belief.

I had internalized a rule that said my body's hunger cues didn't matter—what mattered was the plate being clean. That belief created a pattern. That pattern created a result. And that result triggered shame.

The negative self-talk wasn't addressing the belief. It was punishing me for the consequence of a belief I never chose.

This is why simply replacing negative self-talk with positive affirmations often fails. If the underlying belief remains unchallenged, the new words feel hollow.

Real change required me to trace the self-talk back to its source.

Not: *"Why am I so undisciplined?"* But: *"What belief is driving this behavior?"*

Once I identified the belief—that finishing food was virtuous and wasting it was wrong—I could question it.

Does finishing food I don't need actually help anyone who is starving? Is honoring my body's fullness more important than an empty plate? Once I saw the connection, the belief began to lose its grip.

And as the belief shifted, so did my self-talk. Not through forced positivity, but through clarity.

I was told to take the pill, trust the system, follow the instruction—only to later learn how often symptoms are managed while causes remain untouched.

These beliefs shaped my mindset. That mindset shaped my self-talk.

The reversal began when I stopped obeying the voice and started questioning it.

I recall listening to Bruce Lipton on **a** podcast, and something clicked. He spoke about how people went to their doctor for a cure and instead received a placebo—a sugar pill—then praised the doctor for such a wonder drug. Later, they discovered it had only been a sugar pill. It was the belief in healing, not the pill itself, that created the response.

It reminded me that so much of life is shaped by what we tell ourselves.

CHAPTER 5

Tracing the Voice - Where Negative Self-Talk Begins

Before we can change the voice in our head, we need to understand where it came from.

Negative self-talk doesn't originate with us. It is learned. Absorbed. Internalized from the voices, environments, and experiences that shaped us long before we had the awareness to question them.

Research confirms what many of us intuitively know: the critical voice inside our heads often isn't ours at all. It belongs to someone else, a parent, a teacher, a peer, a culture, a trauma. We simply became the carrier.

The Origins: Where the Voice Was Born

Childhood Criticism and Caregiver Influence

The foundation of our self-talk is laid early. Criticism by caregivers in childhood establishes a negative view of oneself and increases negative self-talk that persists into adulthood. Even well-meaning comments can leave lasting imprints.

The messages we receive in our formative years, both spoken and unspoken, become deeply ingrained in our psyche. A parent's sigh of disappointment. A teacher's public correction. A sibling's comparison. These moments settle into our subconscious and become the soundtrack of our self-perception.

Internalized Abuse and Trauma

Adverse childhood experiences—abuse, neglect, witnessing domestic violence—can make the inner critic particularly loud and unforgiving. The voice becomes a survival mechanism, constantly scanning for danger, anticipating criticism, preparing for rejection.

We carry the voices of those who hurt us, diminished us, or dismissed us. And over time, we no longer need them to speak—we've learned to do it ourselves.

Societal and Cultural Programming

Beyond individual relationships, society itself implants beliefs through cultural norms, media messages, and systemic structures. Social media sets unrealistic standards. Advertisements tell us we're insufficient as we are. Cultural narratives about race, gender, class, and worthiness become internalized as personal truth.

Childhood events such as critical parents or bullying at school plant seeds of self-doubt that grow over time. The habit of negative self-talk often begins when children imitate negative self-talk verbalized by parents or primary caregivers. We learn not just what to think, but how to think about ourselves.

Trauma as a Coping Mechanism

The voice isn't trying to destroy us. It's trying to protect us—using the only tools it learned in survival mode.

The Pattern: How Self-Talk Becomes Automatic

Once these beliefs are established, they become automatic. The subconscious mind operates at approximately 95% capacity by midlife, running programs established in childhood without our conscious awareness.

The critical voice becomes so familiar we mistake it for truth. We don't recognize it as learned programming, we believe it's reality.

The Framework: Tracing Your Voice Back to Its Source

To change negative self-talk, we must first trace it back to its origin. Here is the framework:

Step 1: Catch the Thought

Notice when the critical voice speaks. What does it say? Write it down exactly as you hear it.

Examples:

- "You're going to mess this up."

- "No one wants to hear what you have to say."

- "You should have known better."

- "You're not good enough."

- "Nobody loves me".

Step 2: Identify the Pattern

Ask yourself: When did I first hear this message? Whose voice does this sound like? What situation or person taught me to think this way?

Sometimes the connection is obvious: it's your mother's exact words. Sometimes it's more subtle: it's the tone your teacher used when you made a mistake, now replayed in your own mind.

Step 3: Examine the Evidence

Ask the Socratic questions that cognitive behavioral therapy teaches:

- "Am I having this thought out of habit, or do facts support it?"

- "What evidence do I have that this thought is true?"

- "Are there different interpretations that are more accurate?"

Think of yourself as a lawyer, scientist, or detective. Challenge the thought as if you were defending someone you love—because you are.

Step 4: Reframe with Accuracy

This is not about replacing negative thoughts with unrealistic positive ones. It's about replacing inaccurate, distorted thoughts with balanced, truthful ones.

The Replacements: What to Say Instead

Here are research-backed replacements for common negative self-talk patterns:

Negative Self-Talk   Reframed Self-Talk

- *I'm going to mess up and blow the interview* → I may feel nervous, but I'm qualified for this position and have the ability to do well

- *I'm a failure* → Mistakes happen, and they don't define me. I have many successes to be proud of

- *I'm not good enough* → What evidence do I have that I'm not good enough? Where did this belief come from?

- *I am stupid* → I feel confused about this right now

- *I can't do this* → I'm doing my best" or "This is challenging, and I'm learning

• *Nobody likes me* → Some people connect with me, some don't—and that's normal for everyone

• *I always mess things up* → I made a mistake this time. What can I learn from it?

The Practice: Catch It, Check It, Change It

The UK's National Health Service (NHS) recommends a simple three-step practice:

1. Catch it: Notice the unhelpful thought

2. Check it: Ask if there's evidence supporting it

3. Change it: Reframe the situation with accuracy and self-compassion

For example:

- Catch: "I'm going to fail this presentation."

- Check: "Is there evidence for this? I've prepared thoroughly. I've succeeded before."

- Change: "I'm prepared. I've put in the work, and I'm going to do my best."

The Shift: From Ability to Effort

Research shows that shifting from ability-focused self-talk to effort-focused self-talk is particularly powerful.

Instead of:

- "I'm not smart enough" → "I'll try hard and learn as I go"

- "I'm not talented at this" → "I'll do my very best"

- "I don't have what it takes" → "I'm building the skills I need"

The Truth: You Are Not Your Thoughts

The most important realization in this work is this: You are not your thoughts. You are the observer of your thoughts.

The critical voice is not you. It is programming. It is learned. It is a recording playing on repeat—one you have the power to pause, examine, and replace.

Negative self-talk served a purpose once. It helped you navigate environments that were critical, unsafe, or unpredictable. It tried to keep you small so you wouldn't be hurt. It tried to prepare you for rejection so disappointment wouldn't devastate you.

But you are no longer in that environment. You are no longer that powerless child.

And the voice that once tried to protect you is now limiting you.

Tracing the voice back to its source doesn't erase the past. But it does free you from continuing to live inside it.

When you understand where the voice came from, you can finally choose which voice to listen to now.

CHAPTER 6

When Systems Are Mistaken for Healers

The pattern of inherited belief doesn't stop at the personal level.

It extends to our relationship with institutions—how we are taught to perceive them, trust them, and ultimately surrender to them.

As a society, we hold an unspoken belief that systems are designed to heal, protect, and guide us. We believe the healthcare system heals. The financial system teaches prosperity. The educational system prepares us for life. That belief becomes collective mindset.

But systems are not teachers of truth. They are structures built for specific functions.

The healthcare system is widely believed to be the healer. Yet doctors are not trained to be healers in the holistic sense—they are trained to diagnose, treat symptoms, and manage conditions within defined protocols. Healing, in a deeper sense, is often outside the scope of the system.

This distinction matters.

Just as financial institutions are not designed to teach how money truly works—they are designed to generate profit. Just as the educational system is not built to cultivate wisdom or self-trust, but to standardize knowledge and behavior.

When we mistake systems for saviors, we surrender responsibility.

I saw this clearly while working as a case manager. I worked with a client who had been under psychiatric care for over thirty years. Decades passed, yet nothing fundamentally changed. Around the same time, I reflected on my mother, who had been under the care of a social worker for more than twenty years, moving through the system without meaningful improvement.

The question wasn't why the professionals failed.

The real question was: Why did we believe the system was supposed to heal in the first place?

That belief shapes mindset.

When we believe a system is the authority, our self-talk adapts accordingly:

"Trust the system." "They know better than you." "Don't question it."

This is where self-abandonment begins—not because systems are evil, but because belief replaces awareness.

Once I saw this pattern, it appeared everywhere. In healthcare. In banking. In education. In media. In religion.

Systems do not exist to raise conscious, self-trusting individuals. They exist to function, scale, and sustain themselves.

When we understand this, something powerful happens.

We stop outsourcing our authority. We stop confusing treatment with healing, information with wisdom, and compliance with trust.

That shift doesn't make us defiant.

It makes us accountable.

And accountability is the beginning of choice.

PART II: THE COST

CHAPTER 7

The Cost of Unquestioned Belief

There is a price we pay for beliefs we never examine.

It shows up in our bodies. In our relationships. In opportunities we don't take and dreams we don't pursue. In the exhaustion of living according to rules that were never ours to begin with.

Unquestioned belief doesn't just limit what we think—it limits what we allow ourselves to become.

I didn't realize I was paying this cost for years. I thought the heaviness I felt was just life. The constant second-guessing was caution. The inability to rest was responsibility. The guilt was proof I cared.

But none of that was true.

What I called caution was fear dressed as wisdom. What I called responsibility was perfectionism born from the belief that I had to earn my worth. What I called caring was actually self-abandonment—prioritizing everyone else's expectations over my own well-being.

The cost was invisible because I had been taught it was normal.

When we don't question the beliefs that were never ours to begin with, we leave our lives to chance. We hope it works out. We cross our fingers and trust that what we were told was true, relevant, and still applies.

But hope is not a strategy. And inherited belief is not the same as informed choice.

It takes courage to ask: "Who said so?"

It takes courage to ask: "Where did this information come from?"

It takes courage to ask: "Is this still true today?"

These questions feel like betrayal when we've been taught that loyalty means blind acceptance. But asking these questions is not disrespect—it is discernment.

I remember growing up, we were told to put butter on a burn. It was common knowledge, passed down without question. So when someone got burned, out came the butter. And the burn would blister.

Today, we know that's terrible advice. Butter traps heat increases the risk of infection and makes the injury worse. But back then, no one questioned it. It was what our parents did. What their parents did. Belief was stronger than the evidence.

Even now, some people are so committed to doing things a certain way that facing change feels harder than living with flawed information. Loyalty is not to truth—it's to the source.

"That's how my mother did it." "That's what we've always believed." "That's what I was taught."

And when the source is someone, we love, respect, or depend on, questioning the belief can feel like questioning them. So, we don't. We keep applying butter to the burn—literally and metaphorically—because the belief feels safer than the unknown.

But beliefs are not heirlooms. They are tools.

And when a tool no longer works—or worse, when it causes harm—we have the right to set it down.

This is the cost of unquestioned belief: we continue practices that harm us, avoid opportunities that could heal us, and stay small in spaces that were never designed for our growth—all because we mistake familiarity for truth.

I know this cost personally.

I went for years bowing down to a belief I questioned in the back of my mind. Something did not feel right about my faith, but I didn't have permission to say it out loud—not to others, not even fully to myself.

The questions were always there, quiet and persistent.

Why were books taken out of the Bible? Are those books important? What did they contain that made someone decide they didn't belong? Who made that decision—and why?

These were not rebellious questions. They were honest ones.

But honesty, I learned, is often treated as rebellion when it threatens established belief.

Even now, these questions have to be asked quietly. Raising them can trigger anger and fear in others—not because the questions are wrong, but because years of embedded belief feel like they're being attacked.

When belief becomes identity, questions feel like erasure.

People don't defend the belief itself; they defend what questioning it might cost them. If this belief is wrong, what else might be? If I was misled here, where else have I been misled? If I let go of this, what do I have left?

So, the questions are silenced. Not with answers, but with tone. With disappointment. With warnings about losing faith, straying from the path, being led astray.

But I wasn't being led astray by my questions. I was being led astray by my silence.

The cost of not questioning wasn't peace, it was pretending. It was performing belief I didn't fully hold. It was living with a growing gap between what I was taught to say and what I actually thought.

That gap creates a particular kind of exhaustion. You become two people: the one who asks questions internally, and the one who nods in agreement externally. The split is subtle at first. Then it becomes a chasm.

This is what unexamined belief costs us: our integrity. Our wholeness. The ability to stand in our truth without apology.

And the price only increases the longer we wait.

CHAPTER 8

The Search for Truth

The fact that I questioned my faith caused doubt.

And with doubt came confusion.

For a long time, I thought confusion was the problem. I thought doubt meant something was wrong with me—that I was losing my way, that my faith was weak, that I needed to pray harder or submit more fully.

But confusion wasn't the problem. Confusion was the signal.

It was evidence that something inside me was waking up. That the beliefs I had been given no longer fit the person I was becoming. That the answers I had been handed were no longer answering my actual questions.

So, I went in search of the truth.

I started investigating. Reading what I had been told not to read. Asking questions, I had been taught not to ask. Looking beyond the approved sources, the accepted interpretations, the authorized voices.

And finally, what I found started making sense.

Not the kind of sense that simply confirmed what I already believed—but the kind of sense that clarified why I had been confused in the first place. The pieces began to fit. The contradictions had explanations. The gaps were not gaps in my understanding—they were gaps in what I had been told.

That discovery opened something.

It started a quest: What else had I felt uneasy about? What other beliefs had I secretly questioned but dismissed as doubt?

Once I realized that the truth I had always been told was not the whole truth—not because of malice, but because of limitation—I started questioning everything.

I questioned money. Relationships. Education. Health. Authority. Race. Culture. Success. Safety. Worthiness.

I began to see how deeply we are programmed as a society.

Our families program us. Our churches program us. Our communities, schools, media, and institutions all have a hand in it. We grow up with a mindset about money, relationships, education, race, and culture that we assume is neutral, natural, and true.

Some of it is true. Some of it is helpful. And some of it lingers forever—unchallenged, unexamined, quietly shaping every decision we make.

I had always believed I was not good enough. I had always believed I would never have enough. I had always believed life was full of limits.

These beliefs felt like facts. Like the way things simply were.

But they weren't facts. They were programming.

And programming, I learned, can be rewritten.

What I believe deeply—my embedded beliefs about myself, about life, about what is possible—is based on what I was programmed with as a child. Those beliefs created my mindset. That mindset created my self-talk. And that self-talk became the boundary of what I allowed myself to imagine, attempt, or receive.

But here is what I now know:

We can be reprogrammed.

This is not wishful thinking. It is neuroscience.

Dr. Bruce Lipton's work in epigenetics reinforced what I was discovering: our beliefs literally affect our biology. We are not victims of our genes or our past programming. We have the power to rewrite the code.

Ninety-five percent.

That means most of my life—my reactions, my decisions, my limitations—was being run by programming I didn't choose and had never examined.

Not through pretending. Not through positive affirmations layered over unexamined beliefs. But through the deliberate work of identifying what we were taught, questioning whether it is true, and choosing—consciously—what we will believe moving forward.

This is the work of reprogramming: becoming aware of the operating system, examining the code, and rewriting what no longer serves.

When we change our belief system, we change our lives.

Not because belief is magic, but because belief shapes perception, perception guides decisions, and decisions create outcomes.

The abundant life I was told to pray for was not waiting for me in heaven.

It was waiting for me on the other side of questioning.

PART III: THE REPROGRAMMING

CHAPTER 9

The Work of Reprogramming

Understanding that beliefs can be changed is one thing. Actually changing them is something else entirely.

Reprogramming is not a one-time decision. It is a practice. A discipline. A daily choice to override decades of conditioning with new information, new thoughts, and new patterns.

This is the work I began.

I started meditating. Every morning and every night, I would sit with my eyes closed, focus on my breathing, and intentionally generate elevated emotions—gratitude, joy, love. Not as concepts, but as feelings I allowed my body to experience fully.

I wasn't just thinking positive thoughts. I was reconditioning my nervous system to recognize safety, abundance, and worthiness as the baseline—not the exception.

The "I Am" affirmations became one of the most powerful tools.

I also began listening to pure frequency sounds—432 Hz and higher. Some believe these frequencies can support healing, clarity, and alignment. Whether it was science or the intention behind it, something shifted.

But the deeper work required excavation.

Reprogramming meant examining what I was actually thinking about. Rooting out the fear. The anger. The negative self-talk that had become so automatic I didn't even notice it anymore.

Dr. Joe Dispenza says, *"A memory without the emotional charge is called wisdom."*

That became my goal: to take the charge out of the memories, the phrases, the inherited beliefs—so I could see them clearly and decide what to keep and what to release.

But here's what I also learned: reprogramming doesn't work in isolation.

I realized I had to remove myself from people and environments that would undo what I had accomplished through my reprogramming work.

Not because they were bad people, but because their beliefs were contagious. Their mindset reinforced the old programming I was working so hard to release.

This is one of the hardest parts of transformation: recognizing that some relationships, conversations, and spaces are incompatible with your growth.

You cannot reprogram yourself in the morning and then spend the day surrounded by people reinforcing the old beliefs. The environment matters. The voices you allow into your mind matter. Proximity matters.

Reprogramming is not just about what you think, it's about what you expose yourself to, who you spend time with, and what you allow to influence your subconscious mind.

This work required vigilance. Consistency. And the courage to protect my peace even when it felt isolating.

But slowly, the new beliefs took root.

And the life I was told wasn't possible for me began to unfold.

When Hidden Programming Surfaces

Even now, as I actively work on reprogramming myself, I discover beliefs I didn't know I carried.

Sometimes you can't immediately figure out where the programming originated. The belief is just there, operating in the background, influencing your reactions before you even realize what's happening.

I experienced this recently at a car dealership.

I went to get my tire repaired, and the woman at the service desk told me it would cost $300 for a new tire. I said I just needed the tire patched and plugged —a simple fix. She said that would be $55. Fine. So they took my car back to the serve area for the fix.

A little while later, the woman returned and said, *"We found a nail in your tire and we'll fix it."* Then a few minutes later she came back again and said, *"We have a problem. We discovered a second nail in the tire."* Okay, how much will that cost? She said, *"Please come with me. I want to show it to you."*

She explained that one of the nails was lodged in the tire in such a way that it could not be repaired. At that point I said, *"So now I have to buy a new tire? Y'all just put that nail in there so I would have to spend $300."*

She repeated my exact words back to me, and it sounded so ridiculous.

But the belief had already spoken.

I left the dealership so embarrassed. Where did that thinking come from? The automatic distrust. The assumption that I was being scammed. The certainty that they were lying to take advantage of me.

I examined it.

And there it was: my community. My culture.

Many African American people have been lied to—by government, corporations, healthcare systems, housing authorities, and the media. Repeatedly. Systemically. For generations.

The distrust wasn't irrational. It was inherited. It was learned through experience—not mine personally, but the collective experience of people who look like me. People who were told they were getting one thing and received another. People who were promised fairness and got exploitation. People who learned the system was not designed to be honest with them.

That belief had been sitting inside me, quietly shaping how I moved through the world.

And I had no idea it was there.

It had been affecting me all along—in ways I hadn't recognized. How many times had I assumed the worst before giving someone a chance? How many opportunities had I approached with suspicion instead of openness? How many interactions had been filtered through this lens of distrust?

So it is worth noting that even though my work had begun, I discovered there was still much more hidden within the distorted beliefs I had inherited from my community.

The Deeper Layer: Distrust Within My Own Community

But there's another layer to this distrust that's even more insidious.

In my culture as an African American, one belief that has been distorted is that Black people cannot be trusted to do a professional job.

In many conversations with my people, we acknowledge that Black people are more than qualified to build, produce, invent, and grow. History—including places like Black Wall Street in Tulsa—has proven our abilities. We know our achievements have often been ignored or distorted.

Yet there is still an underlying belief.

I often hear Black people say, *"I'm going to take my business to the white man."*

I have been guilty of thinking this way, and many of my own family feel this way. And oh by the way my grandfather was notorious for saying, "the white man ain't never gone let you have anything."

Without knowing where this belief came from, the contradiction is astounding.

We know our history. We know what we're capable of. We talk about supporting Black businesses, economic empowerment, and building wealth within our community.

This belief didn't come from our capability. It came from centuries of systematic devaluation—from being told we weren't good enough, smart enough, or professional enough. From being excluded from opportunities, education, and resources—and then blamed for the very gaps that exclusion created.

And the cruelest part? We internalized it.

The oppressor's voice became our own.

This is how inherited beliefs destroy communities—not only through overt oppression, but through the quiet, unconscious choices we make every single day, without realizing we are perpetuating the very system that harmed us.

This is what reprogramming requires us to see. Not just the belief—but who planted it, why it was planted, and who continues to benefit from us believing it.

This is the ongoing work: catching these invisible beliefs as they surface, tracing them back to their origin, and deciding whether they still belong in my operating system.

Some days I catch them. Some days I don't.

But the more aware I become, the more choice I have.

And choice is freedom

CHAPTER 10

Acting As If

There comes a moment in reprogramming when you have to put action behind the belief.

Not because you're certain. Not because you have proof. But because belief without aligned action remains theoretical.

For me, that moment came when I quit my job as a case manager.

No backup plan. No other income. Just a decision that if I was going to truly internalize what I had started to believe about abundance, worthiness, and possibility—I had to act as if it were already true.

I remember hearing something on YouTube that stopped me in my tracks. I wrote it down. At first, I had to read it several times a day just to keep the belief alive. But eventually, I memorized it. It became part of me.

This is the quote:

"I am so happy and grateful for the fact that I am now (fill-in the blank with what you want)

I am.

I want to emphasize how important and powerful the "I Am" statements are. Whenever you attach "I AM" to any word, it becomes deeply internalized and you often attract more of what you connect it to.

So, for example, if you say, "I am broke," you may begin to embody the mindset, habits, and emotions connected to lack—and attract more of the same.

In contrast, if you say, "I am worthy," the same principle can apply. You begin to align with thoughts, choices, and behaviors that reflect worthiness.

When you say "I am" to something, you're not just describing yourself — you're reinforcing a neural pattern. Every time you say it, think it, or act on it, you're strengthening that pathway. Your identity is literally encoded in the structure of your brain as a collection of self-referential neural patterns, and your brain treats your identity as ground truth — the foundation of its predictive model. Substack

Your subconscious mind doesn't argue; it just obeys. It takes "I AM" statements as commands and finds proof to make them true. You're training your brain through repetition, the same way you learned your name, your language, and your habits. Rob Dial

I examine my thoughts. I ask: Is this true? Where did this come from? Does this serve who I am now?

And then—this is the crucial part—I replace it with what I want.

Not what I don't want. Not what I'm afraid of. Not what I've been conditioned to expect.

What I want.

This is huge.

For most of my life, my thoughts were consumed with what I didn't want. What I was trying to avoid. What I feared would happen. And my subconscious mind, operating at 95% capacity, delivered exactly what I focused on. "95% of the day, our life is coming straight out of the programs in our subconscious." — Bruce Lipton Fearless Soul

Now, I focus on what I want. And my mind, my actions, my decisions align accordingly.

The work I am doing is amazing.

Not because I've arrived at some final destination, but because I've learned how to navigate. I've learned how to recognize inherited beliefs, question them, and replace them with beliefs that actually serve my growth.

I've learned that transformation is not about becoming someone new—it's about unbecoming everything that was never truly you in the first place.

And what remains is not fragile positivity or hollow affirmations.

What remains is power. Clarity. Freedom.

The freedom to choose what I believe. The freedom to act from that belief. The freedom to create a life that reflects my truth—not someone else's programming.

This is what reprogramming offers: not a perfect life, but a conscious one.

Not the absence of challenges, but the presence of choice.

And that choice changes everything.

PART IV: THE BELIEF SYSTEMS

CHAPTER 11

Money - From Scarcity to Abundance

Money was never just about money.

It was about worthiness. Safety. Possibility. Freedom. Power.

And for most of my life, the beliefs I held about money determined how much of it I allowed myself to have, keep, and grow.

But circumstances are shaped by decisions. And decisions are shaped by beliefs.

The beliefs I inherited about money were rooted in scarcity. Not because my family was unkind or ignorant, but because scarcity was their reality—and their programming.

The Programming: What I Was Taught

"Money don't grow on trees"

"We can't afford it"

"Do you think I'm made of money"

"We are just scrapping by"

"I have to rob Peter to pay Paul"

"We don't have enough"

"Money is the root of all evil"

"Another day another dollar"

These phrases weren't just statements. They were beliefs about how the world works, what was possible for people like us, and what money meant.

I absorbed these beliefs without question. Money was scarce. Money was hard to get. Money required struggle. And even if you got it, it wouldn't last.

These beliefs shaped my relationship with money for decades.

The Scarcity Mindset: How It Shows Up

A scarcity mindset isn't just about not having enough money. It's about believing there will never be enough—no matter how much you have.

Here's how scarcity thinking manifests:

Money

- Scarcity mindset short-term goals, at best, or none at all. They tend to live paycheck to paycheck.

- They are trapped in the "earn-and-spend" cycle, where money is seen as something to be earned from a job and then spent, rather than invested.

- They work for money and have an active income mindset: work one time, get paid one time.

- Scarcity mindset is associated with a very near-term focus—more concerned with meeting immediate needs than planning for the future or saving for long-term goals.

- Hoarding tendencies emerge because of a root belief that money is scarce and fleeting.

This was me. I worked for the next paycheck. I paid the bills. I hoped there'd be enough left over. I never thought about wealth building because wealth felt like something other people had access to—not me.

Career

- Scarcity mindset, work for their next paycheck. You work to pay the bills. You put in more time; you get more money. Then you get more bills, and the golden handcuffs take hold.

- The mindset is to manage finances defensively, continually doing whatever is necessary to pay the bills. While the wealthy are actively playing to win, the poor are playing not to lose.

- Poor people choose to play the role of victim. Instead of taking responsibility for what's going on in their lives, they choose "poor me" thinking.

Relationships

- Reluctance to leave toxic relationships, driven by fear that you lack other options.

- Unreasonable demands on time and attention from partners, friends, or family, anything less than "full-time" attention feels unsatisfactory.

- The scarcity mindset believes the world is one giant pie. Every time you help someone or share what you have, others will be getting a piece and there will be one less piece for you.

- Scarcity mindset people hoard and struggle with sharing profit, power, recognition, and credit. They keep thoughts and plans to themselves, fearing ideas might be stolen or result in personal failure.

I see this now. The fear of sharing ideas. The hesitation to celebrate others' success because it felt like their gain was my loss. The belief that if someone else won, it meant less for me.

Family and Community

- If your parents or caregivers had a scarcity mindset due to financial struggles, they may have focused much of their attention on meeting financial needs, leaving less room for emotional presence, creativity, or possibility.

- A scarcity mindset in the home teaches children that giving costs something significant—and that cost often outweighs the benefit.

I remember hearing conversations about what we couldn't do, where we couldn't go, what we couldn't afford. The message wasn't just about money—it was about limits. Life had limits. Dreams had limits. We had limits.

And I internalized those limits as truth.

The Core Difference: Scarcity vs. Abundance

The difference between a scarcity mindset and an abundance mindset isn't about how much money you have. It's about how you see the world.

Scarcity asks: "Why is this happening to me?" Abundance asks: "What opportunity does this create?"

Scarcity believes: The world is one giant pie—if someone else gets a piece, there's less for me. Abundance believes: There isn't just one pie. There are many. Giving doesn't deplete—it expands.

Scarcity thinks: I have to protect what I have because it might not come back. Abundance thinks: The world is an expandable place. There's more where that came from. Resources can replenish. Generosity isn't foolish.

Scarcity lives: As if you are always five minutes away from ruin. It hoards affection, opportunity, and resources. Abundance lives: Believing that mistakes aren't fatal, that resources can be rebuilt, and that giving strengthens rather than depletes.

This shift in perspective changes everything.

The Wealth Mindset: How the Rich Think Differently

Research on wealth-building consistently shows that rich people think differently—not because they're smarter or more deserving, but because they hold different beliefs.

Money

- The rich understand a simple principle: money makes money, and the money that money makes, makes money. (This is compound wealth-building.)

- They see money not as an end, but as a means to create more value and wealth.

- They are not afraid of debt—they use it strategically to invest and expand their wealth.

- The rich invest in passive income. They work one time and make money over and over again.

- They are more likely to take calculated risks because they have diversified assets and see opportunity where others see danger.

Career

- The wealthy work to learn. They grow their skills and abilities and continually rise up the ranks.

- The biggest compounded return comes from education. Most millionaires in the United States were not born millionaires—they learned how to build wealth.

- Those with a "rich mindset" see wealth as a result of creating value in the lives of others. By focusing on solving problems and meeting needs, they contribute positively to society while also reaping the rewards.

Relationships

- Your network is your net worth." Those with wealth connect with other people intentionally. Rich people are deliberate about the friends they keep.

- People with an abundance mindset believe giving is a heartfelt desire to serve others and is rooted in wholeheartedness—not obligation or depletion.

- An abundance mindset isn't just about giving. It's about seeing the people around you: their needs, their strengths, and the possibilities that emerge from who they are and who they can become.

- Someone with an abundance mindset sees mentoring as an investment that strengthens the whole team and ultimately benefits everyone, including themselves.

- Instead of hiring help for everything, teach children domestic skills. Show them that giving costs something, but that cost is relatively small and comes with invisible, immeasurable benefits that ripple far beyond the kitchen.

- Community has a compounding effect. Saying yes to opportunities, seeing needs, and recognizing possibilities creates exponential growth.

- Teaching children to share when they are two is easy—but do we maintain that momentum when they are fifteen?

My Shift: From Scarcity to Abundance

The shift began when I recognized that my beliefs about money were not facts—they were programming.

I started questioning:

- Is it true that money is scarce, or is that just what I was taught?

- Is it true that rich people are greedy, or is that a belief designed to keep me from pursuing wealth?

- Is it true that I have to struggle for every dollar, or is that a belief rooted in my grandfather's experience—not mine?

Once I questioned the beliefs, I could examine them.

And once I examined them, I could replace them.

Old Belief: Money doesn't grow on trees.

New Belief: Money is a tool that multiplies when invested wisely.

Old Belief: We can't afford it.

New Belief: How can I create the resources to afford it?

Old Belief: Rich people are greedy.

New Belief: Wealth is created by adding value to others' lives.

Old Belief: I have to work hard for every dollar.

New Belief: I can work smart and create systems that generate passive income.

Old Belief: If someone else wins, there's less for me.

New Belief: Someone else's success doesn't diminish my opportunity. There is room for all of us to thrive.

This wasn't just positive thinking. This was re-programming backed by action.

This isn't just anecdotal. Research consistently shows that mindset shapes financial outcomes.

Robert Kiyosaki's Rich Dad Poor Dad laid the foundation for understanding that financial education isn't taught in schools—and that the beliefs we inherit about money often keep us trapped in cycles of scarcity.

For a long time, I felt guilty for wanting to be rich, even now the phrase sounds foreign to me. I can still hear my mother saying, "I don't ever want to be rich."

The key is this: wealthy people are clear about wanting wealth. They are unwavering in their desire. They are fully committed to creating wealth. Poor people, on the other hand, often think they're doomed to remain in poverty. They believe the lie that most millionaires inherited their wealth—when in fact, most built it through learning, risk-taking, and belief in possibility.

The Cost of Scarcity Thinking

Scarcity thinking doesn't just limit your bank account. It limits your life.

It causes:

- Hyper fixation on immediate problems, leaving no mental space for long-term solutions.

- Short-term coping instead of long-term problem-solving.

- Increased resentfulness and stress, because others' success feels threatening.

- Hoarding of resources, ideas, and opportunities, which blocks growth and connection.

- Living emotionally as if you are always five minutes away from ruin, even when you're not.

This was the cost I paid for years. The exhaustion of always playing defense. The resentfulness that came from believing there wasn't enough to go around. The fear that kept me small.

The Freedom of Abundance Thinking

When you shift from scarcity to abundance, you don't just change your relationship with money, you change your relationship with life.

Abundance thinking allows you to:

- See opportunity instead of threat.

- Collaborate instead of competing.

- Give freely because you trust more will come.

- Take calculated risks because failure is feedback, not finality.

- Build wealth that serves not just you, but your family, your community, and your legacy.

Abundance isn't about having more. It's about believing more is possible.

And when you believe it—and act from that belief—it becomes true.

The Invitation: Examine Your Money Beliefs

If you grew up hearing "we can't afford it," pause and ask:

- What belief did that teach me about money?

- Is that belief still serving me, or is it limiting me?

If you were taught that rich people are greedy, ask:

- Where did that belief come from?

- Does it serve my growth, or does it keep me from pursuing wealth?

If you believe you have to struggle for every dollar, ask:

- Is that true, or is that inherited programming?

- What would happen if I believed money could flow with ease?

Your beliefs about money are not permanent. They are not facts. They are programming—and programming can be rewritten.

An abundant life isn't reserved for other people.

It's available to anyone willing to question the scarcity beliefs they inherited and consciously choose abundance instead.

Money doesn't grow on trees.

But wealth grows in the mind that believes it can.

CHAPTER 12

Health - From Compliance to Body Wisdom

The beliefs I held about my body shaped how I treated it.

For years, I believed my body was something to control, override, and manage. I believed doctors had the answers and my job was to comply. I believed symptoms were problems to suppress rather than signals to understand. I believed my body was separate from my mind—that what I thought had little to do with what I felt physically.

All of those beliefs were wrong.

And they cost me my health.

The Programming: What I Was Taught About My Body

These weren't just instructions. They were beliefs about authority, compliance, and who gets to decide what happens to your body.

By adulthood, I had learned to ignore my body completely.

I didn't question it. Because I had been taught not to question medical authority.

But something inside me knew there had to be another way.

The Awakening: My Body Had Been Trying to Speak

The diabetes diagnosis was a turning point.

Not because I accepted it—but because I finally started questioning it.

I began researching. I learned that Type 2 diabetes, in many cases, is reversible through diet and lifestyle changes. I learned that my body wasn't broken—it was responding to what I was putting into it.

So I changed what I ate. I stopped overriding my body's hunger and fullness cues. I started listening instead of controlling.

And my diabetes reversed.

Not because of a miracle. Not because I got lucky. But because I stopped treating my body like an enemy to be managed and started treating it like an intelligent system that knew what it needed.

When I told that woman at the doctor's office that I had reversed my diabetes through diet, she said her doctor didn't believe it could be reversed. So he kept prescribing medication.

Her final words: "I trust my doctor."

And I understood. Because I had been her. I had surrendered my authority to someone with credentials, assuming they knew my body better than I did.

But they didn't.

The Science: Your Mind Can Make You Sick—Or Heal You

What I discovered through my own experience, science has confirmed.

Dr. Bruce Lipton and Dr. Joe Dispenza have both dedicated their careers to understanding the connection between thoughts, beliefs, and physical health. And their research reveals something profound: your thoughts cause biochemical reactions that affect every cell in your body.

Fear and Survival Mode Create Disease

This is what happens when your self-talk is rooted in fear:

- "I'm not safe."

- "I can't trust anyone."

- "Something bad is going to happen."

- "I'm always one step away from disaster."

Your body hears those thoughts. And it responds by flooding your system with stress hormones—cortisol, adrenaline, norepinephrine—preparing you for a threat that may not even exist.

And when that state becomes chronic, disease follows.

Gratitude and Growth Create Healing

The opposite is also true.

This is the power of reprogramming your self-talk from fear to gratitude:

Fear-based self-talk produces:

- Cortisol (stress hormone)

- Adrenaline (survival mode)

- Suppressed immune function

- Chronic inflammation

- Disease

Gratitude-based self-talk produces:

- Serotonin (mood stabilizer)

- Endorphins (natural pain relief)

- Human growth hormone (repair and healing)

- Enhanced immune function

- Health

Your thoughts are not neutral. They are instructions to your body.

The Cost of Compliance: When You Abandon Your Body

For years, I lived in survival mode without realizing it.

I was constantly stressed. Constantly vigilant. Constantly preparing for the worst. My self-talk reflected that:

Those thoughts weren't just mental. They were chemical.

Every time I thought them, my body flooded with cortisol. Every time I believed them, my immune system weakened. Every time I reinforced them, my body moved further from healing and closer to disease.

And I didn't know it. Because I had been taught to ignore my body's signals.

So I complied. I ate when I wasn't hungry. I ignored fullness. I overrode discomfort. I pushed through exhaustion. I medicated symptoms instead of examining causes.

And my body paid the price.

The diabetes wasn't random. It was the result of years of ignoring what my body was trying to tell me. Years of stress hormones. Years of inflammatory foods. Years of believing my body was something to control rather than something to listen to.

The Shift: From Compliance to Body Wisdom

The reversal began when I stopped complying and started listening.

I stopped finishing everything on my plate just because it was there. I stopped eating past fullness out of guilt. I stopped taking medications without questioning them. I stopped assuming doctors knew my body better than I did.

And I started asking my body what it needed.

Not what I was told it needed. Not what the system said it needed. What it actually needed.

And it answered.

It told me when it was full. It told me what foods made it feel heavy. It told me when it needed rest. It told me when stress was becoming chronic.

And when I listened—really listened—my health transformed.

The diabetes reversed. The weight came off. The constant fatigue lifted. Not because I forced my body into submission, but because I finally gave it permission to heal.

The Research: The Placebo Effect Is Real

This isn't "woo-woo." This is documented science.

Your belief about whether you will heal influences whether you actually heal.

If you believe the medication will work, it's more likely to work. If you believe your body can heal, it's more likely to heal. If you believe you're doomed to be sick, you're more likely to stay sick.

This means your self-talk about your health is not passive commentary. It is active programming.

The New Self-Talk: From Fear to Healing

I had to change the way I spoke to and about my body.

Old Self-Talk (Fear-Based):

-   "My body is broken."

-   "I'll always struggle with my weight."

-   "I'm diabetic—this is permanent."

-   "I can't trust my body."

New Self-Talk (Healing-Based):

- "My body knows how to heal."

- "I trust my body's signals."

- "My body is responding to what I give it."

- "Health is my natural state."

This wasn't positive thinking for the sake of feeling good. This was reprogramming for the sake of survival.

Because when you live in fear-based self-talk, your body stays in survival mode. And survival mode shuts down healing.

But when you shift to gratitude-based, healing-focused self-talk, your body shifts into growth mode. And growth mode is where healing happens.

The Practice: Gratitude as Medicine

Dr. Dispenza teaches that you don't wait to feel gratitude after you're healed. You feel gratitude as if you're already healed—and that feeling creates the biochemical environment for healing to occur.

I started practicing this daily.

Every morning and every night, I meditated. Not to escape my body, but to connect with it. I focused on gratitude—not for what I hoped would happen, but for what I was choosing to believe was already happening.

At first, it felt like lying. Because my body didn't feel healed yet. But I kept practicing.

And over time, something shifted.

The gratitude stopped feeling forced. The healing stopped feeling distant. My body started responding—not because I tricked it, but because I stopped programming it with fear and started programming it with possibility.

The Invitation: Listen to Your Body

Your body has been trying to speak to you your entire life.

It told you when you were full, but you were taught to ignore it. It told you when you were tired, but you were taught to push through. It told you when something was wrong, but you were taught to medicate the symptom and move on.

What if you stopped ignoring it?

What if you stopped treating your body like an inconvenience and started treating it like the intelligent system it is?

What if you asked your body what it needed—and then actually listened?

Your body is not your enemy. It never was.

It's been trying to protect you, guide you, and heal you all along.

The question is: Are you ready to listen?

Reflection Questions:

What beliefs do you hold about your body?

Where did those beliefs come from?

How does your self-talk about your health sound? Is it rooted in fear or trust?

What would change if you believed your body was capable of healing?

Health is not just about what you eat or how much you exercise.

It's about what you believe.

And belief creates biology.

CHAPTER 13

Relationships - From Herd Mentality to Self-Approval

For most of my life, my relationships were shaped and molded by others.

Perceptions and beliefs about what I should do to be accepted. What I should buy to be respected. What I should say to be liked. How I should act to belong.

It didn't come from me. It came from the herd.

And for years, I followed without realizing I was following.

The Herd: How Beliefs Dictate Relationships

Herd mentality is the tendency for people's behavior or beliefs to conform to those of the group they belong to. It's not new. It's evolutionary. Early humans survived by sticking together—safety in numbers, strength in conformity.

But what helped us survive as a species can limit us as individuals.

Research shows that it takes only 5% of individuals to influence the remaining 95% of a group, who follow without realizing it. We conform not because we've examined the behavior and decided it's right—but because others are doing it, and doing what others do feels safer than standing alone.

This shows up everywhere:

In what we buy. In how we dress. In what we say we believe. In who we pretend to be.

And for many of us, it shows up in relationships—not just with others, but with ourselves.

The Beliefs That Shaped My Relationships

I grew up with beliefs about how relationships were supposed to work:

These beliefs weren't about connection. They were about performance.

And I performed.

I spent money I didn't have to look like I had it together. I dressed to impress people whose opinions didn't actually matter. I stayed quiet when I wanted to speak. I agreed when I wanted to question. I smiled when I felt uncomfortable.

All because I believed that my value was determined by how others saw me.

The Root: Not Feeling Good Enough

Here's what I've come to understand: the need to impress others is rooted in not feeling good about yourself.

When you don't believe you're enough as you are, you try to make others believe you're enough. You perform worthiness instead of embodying it.

You buy the car to prove success. You wear the outfit to prove status. You stay silent to prove you're not a problem. You agree to prove you're easy to be around.

But none of it works. Because approval from others can never fill the gap created by your own disapproval of yourself.

I see this clearly now. The relationships I stayed in that weren't healthy. The friendships I maintained that drained me. The environments I tolerated limited me.

I stayed because I believed:

The herd felt safer than the unknown. Even when the herd was toxic.

The Science: Why We Conform

The famous Asch conformity experiments in the 1950s revealed just how powerful herd mentality is.

In the study, a single participant was placed in a room with seven actors who had been instructed to give the wrong answer to a simple visual test. Even though the correct answer was obvious, 75% of participants conformed to the group's incorrect answer at least once.

When asked why, participants said they didn't want to stand out. They didn't want to be wrong. They didn't want to be judged.

This is what herd mentality does: it makes us change our values or beliefs to gain approval from the group rather than endure judgment or criticism.

Peer pressure—whether overt or subtle—reinforces conformity, nudging individuals toward collective behavior in a bid to secure belonging and validation.

And it doesn't just affect what we say. It affects what we buy, how we dress, who we date, where we work, and how we see ourselves.

The Cost: Living for Others' Approval

Living for others' approval costs you your integrity.

When identity is built on conformity, you become whoever the group needs you to be. You lose touch with what you actually want, believe, or value. You perform a version of yourself that gets approved—but it's not actually you.

Research shows that when people care about their status, conformity helps them maintain it, while departing from social norms carries the risk of impaired status. Reputation survives a loss better if others are losing at the same time.

This is why people stay in jobs they hate, relationships that drain them, and belief systems they've outgrown. Leaving feels riskier than staying—even when staying costs them their peace.

I lived this for years.

I stayed in environments where I didn't belong because leaving meant facing the question: What if I'm not accepted somewhere else?

I performed a version of myself that was palatable, likable, non-threatening —because the alternative felt like rejection.

But the cost was enormous. I was exhausted. Resentful. Disconnected from myself.

And I didn't even realize it—because everyone around me was doing the same thing.

The Shift: When You Stop Caring What Others Think

The shift didn't happen all at once. It happened in small moments of clarity.

The moment I realized I was dressing for people I didn't even like. The moment I caught myself agreeing with something I didn't believe just to avoid conflict. The moment I saw how much energy I was spending trying to manage other people's perceptions of me.

And the biggest moment: when I realized that the people whose approval I was chasing didn't actually know me. They knew the performance. And the performance was exhausting.

So I stopped.

Not all at once. Not perfectly. But progressively.

I stopped buying things to impress people. I stopped staying in conversations that felt performative. I stopped pretending to agree when I didn't. I stopped explaining myself to people who weren't trying to understand me.

And something remarkable happened.

The people who were only there for the performance left. And I didn't miss them.

The relationships that were built on conformity faded. And I felt lighter.

The spaces that required me to be small became uncomfortable. And I stopped going.

What remained were relationships built on authenticity, not approval.

The Freedom: Not Needing External Validation

When you are no longer concerned with what others think, it is a sign of growth.

Not because you've become arrogant or uncaring—but because you've stopped outsourcing your sense of worth.

You stop needing others to validate your choices. You stop performing to prove your value. You stop shrinking to make others comfortable.

This doesn't mean you don't care about people. It means you stop letting their opinions dictate your decisions.

I see myself just fine now. And that's the difference.

I don't need others to see me the way I see myself. I don't need their approval to feel worthy. I don't need their validation to know I'm on the right path.

This is freedom.

Not the absence of relationships—but the presence of authentic ones. Relationships where I show up as I am, not as I think I should be.

The Reprogramming: From Herd to Self

The work of reprogramming my relationship beliefs looked like this:

Old Belief: "I need to impress people to be accepted."

New Belief: "The right people accept me as I am."

Old Belief: "What will people think?"

New Belief: "What do I think?"

Old Belief: "I have to keep the peace, even if it costs me my voice."

New Belief: "Peace without honesty isn't peace—it's performance."

Old Belief: "If I don't conform, I'll be rejected."

New Belief: "If I have to conform to belong, I don't actually belong."

Old Belief: "I'm not good enough, so I need others to validate me."

New Belief: "I am enough. My worth isn't determined by others' opinions."

This shift didn't just change my relationships with others. It changed my relationship with myself.

I stopped abandoning myself to please the herd. I stopped performing worthiness and started embodying it. I stopped seeking approval and started trusting my own discernment.

The Research: Breaking Free from Conformity

Breaking free from herd mentality requires cultivating critical thinking.

The willingness to think independently doesn't just benefit the individual —it benefits the collective. It creates space for innovation, diversity, and truth.

But it requires courage.

It requires the ability to question assumptions, evaluate sources, and entertain diverse perspectives. It requires self-reflection, seeking dissenting viewpoints, and challenging prevailing narratives.

And most importantly, it requires the willingness to stand alone when necessary.

Not because you're against people—but because you're for truth.

The Danger of Permanent Conformity

Unchecked conformity doesn't just limit the individual—it limits the group.

When everyone is following, no one is leading. When everyone is performing, no one is authentic. When everyone is afraid to question, error becomes truth simply because no one challenges it.

History shows us the dangers: mass hysteria, financial bubbles, totalitarian regimes—all illustrating the perils of blind allegiance to the collective.

The suppression of dissent not only stifles progress but creates fertile ground for misinformation and manipulation.

This is why questioning the herd isn't rebellious—it's responsible.

Where I Am Now

By doing this reprogramming work, I have come a long way.

I am no longer concerned about how others see me. I see me just fine.

I don't dress to impress. I dress for myself. I don't spend money I don't have to prove something I don't need to prove. I don't stay in relationships that require me to shrink. I don't perform a version of myself that isn't real.

And the result?

I have fewer relationships—but they're real. I have less approval—but I have more peace. I have less performance—but I have more freedom.

The herd kept me safe once. But it also kept me small.

And I'm no longer willing to stay small to belong.

Reflection Questions

Which relationships in your life are built on performance rather than authenticity?

What beliefs do you hold about needing others' approval?

Where did those beliefs come from?

What would change if you stopped caring what "they" think?

Who would you become if you gave yourself permission to leave the herd?

The herd is not your home. It's just where you learned to survive.

But you're not just surviving anymore.

You're becoming.

CHAPTER 14

Identity - From Programmed Self to Authentic Self

Identity is not something we are born knowing. It is something we are taught to perform.

Long before we learn who we are, we learn who we are allowed to be. Identity forms quietly in the background of childhood—through tone, labels, expectations, praise, correction, and comparison. By the time we can name ourselves, we are already answering to descriptions that were never fully ours.

Identity is belief made personal.

What you believe about yourself determines how you introduce yourself, how you explain yourself, and how you defend yourself. It shapes what you say out loud to others and what you repeat silently to yourself.

These are not facts. They are conclusions.

Programming Happens Before Choice

In our early years, we don't have the power to question what we are told. We absorb.

We learn who we are through:

What is rewarded What is criticized What is ignored What is expected

None of these identities are accidental.

They are survival strategies turned into personality traits.

Programming teaches us not just how to behave, but how to describe ourselves. Over time, those descriptions harden into identity. And once identity forms, mindset follows.

My Programmed Identities

I carried many identities I never chose.

These identities weren't lies—they were adaptations. They helped me survive environments that required me to be strong, responsible, and self-limiting.

But survival identities are not growth identities.

And at some point, I had to ask: Who am I protecting by staying this version of myself?

Mindset Is Identity in Motion

Mindset is how identity thinks.

Mindset doesn't exist independently—it serves identity.

And identity speaks.

It speaks when you explain why you didn't apply. It speaks when you justify staying. It speaks when you downplay your desires. It speaks when you tell someone who you are before they ever ask.

What you say about yourself to others is often a mirror of what you say to yourself when no one is listening.

For years, my mindset reflected my programmed identity:

That mindset wasn't wrong given the identity I was operating from. But it kept me in a constant state of defense. I was always bracing for impact. Always preparing for disappointment. Always protecting myself from a world I believed was designed to limit me.

And that mindset created a life that matched it.

Self-Talk: The Private Performance of Identity

Self-talk is identity rehearsing.

It is the quiet reinforcement of who you believe yourself to be. And because identity was formed before conscious choice, self-talk often feels automatic, reasonable, and true.

"I'm just being realistic." "This is how I've always been." "People like me don't do that."

But realism is often just repetition.

Self-talk doesn't ask whether an identity is accurate—it asks whether it is familiar. And familiarity feels safe, even when it is limiting.

This is why changing habits without addressing identity rarely lasts. The moment a new behavior threatens the old identity, the mind intervenes.

"This isn't you." "Who do you think you are?" "Don't get ahead of yourself."

That voice is not sabotage. It is protection—of an outdated identity.

I see this now in my own journey. When I quit my job as a case manager to pursue real estate, my self-talk immediately challenged my new identity:

The voice wasn't trying to destroy me. It was trying to keep me inside the identity I had always known: the responsible one. The cautious one. The one who doesn't rock the boat.

But that identity couldn't take me where I wanted to go.

Who Are You Without the Programming?

One of the most uncomfortable questions we can ask is this:

Who would I be if I stopped introducing myself through my limitations?

For many of us, identity is intertwined with struggle. It becomes familiar. It becomes part of how we relate to others. Sometimes it even becomes how we receive validation.

When identity is built on endurance, letting go of struggle can feel like betrayal. When identity is built on responsibility, choosing ease can feel irresponsible. When identity is built on being needed, choosing yourself can feel selfish.

But growth requires disidentification.

Not erasing who you've been—but loosening your grip on who you were taught to be.

I had to ask myself:

These questions didn't feel empowering at first. They felt destabilizing.

Because when you've spent your whole life performing an identity, questioning it feels like losing yourself.

But you're not losing yourself. You're finding yourself underneath the costume.

Reclaiming Identity Is an Inside Job

Reclaiming identity does not begin with announcing a new version of yourself to the world. It begins privately, in the way you speak to yourself.

Instead of asking: "Who am I supposed to be?"

Ask: "What did I learn to believe about myself?"

What beliefs shaped the identity you've been performing? What roles did you step into because they were rewarded? What labels did you accept because they explained your pain?

For me, the process looked like this:

Identity changes when belief changes.

And belief changes when you allow yourself to question the story you've been telling—about who you are, what you're capable of, and what is possible for you.

The Identity Shift in Action

When I got my real estate license at age 66, I didn't just change careers. I changed identities.

That shift—from performing a limited identity to embodying an abundant one—changed everything.

Because identity determines action.

But I chose a new identity. And then I acted as if it were already true.

And it became true.

Not because I pretended. But because I stopped performing the old identity and started living from the new one.

Reflection: Examining Your Programmed Identity

Take a moment to ask yourself:

How do you usually describe yourself to others?

Which parts of that description feel inherited rather than chosen?

What identity did you adopt to stay safe, loved, or accepted?

Who might you become if you questioned that identity?

These are not easy questions. They require honesty. They require letting go of descriptions you've worn for so long they feel like skin.

But identity is not discovered—it is examined.

And when belief shifts, identity loosens. When identity loosens, mindset expands. When mindset expands, self-talk softens.

And in that space, something real finally has room to emerge.

The Freedom of Undefined Identity

Here is what I've learned: You don't have to know exactly who you are to stop being who you were told to be.

You don't need a fully formed new identity to release the old one.

You just need permission to question. To pause. To say, "I don't know if that's true anymore."

The most powerful identity is the one that allows you to evolve.

Not the one that keeps you fixed. Not the one that explains your limitations. Not the one that makes others comfortable.

The one that gives you permission to grow.

Identity is not your prison. It never was.

It was just the costume you wore to survive.

And now, you get to choose what you wear next.

Or better yet—you get to choose to stop performing altogether.

CHAPTER 15

Faith - From Inherited Religion to Personal Spirituality

Religion, belief, and spirituality is a very sensitive subject.

I know this because I've lived it. I've questioned it. And I've experienced the anger, fear, and stress that comes when deeply held beliefs are scrutinized.

This chapter is not about changing your mind. It's not about convincing you of anything. It's about sharing my journey—from inherited religion to personal spirituality—and inviting you to judge whether the beliefs you hold about faith are truly yours, or whether they were simply handed down.

The Journey: From Catholic to Baptist to Seeker

For years, I was raised Catholic.

I learned the prayers. I attended mass. I followed the rituals. And I believed what I was told to believe—because that's what you do when you're young. You don't question. You absorb.

Later, I briefly dated a Muslim. I was exposed to a different tradition, different practices, different names for the same search: connection to something greater.

Then I became a Baptist. New church. New doctrine. New rules. But still, the same pattern: believe what you're told, don't question too deeply, and trust that those in authority know better than you.

But even as a 15-year-old, something in me was searching beyond the boundaries of organized religion.

I created experiments related to pyramid power—trying to understand energy, resonance, and forces I couldn't see but could sense. I briefly got into astrology, fascinated by patterns, cycles, and the idea that there was a larger design at work.

And beneath all of it was a persistent question: Where did I come from? And why am I here?

The Foundation: Be Transformed by the Renewing of Your Mind

In all those years of religious instruction, one verse kept showing up—though I didn't fully understand its power until much later.

Romans 12:2: "Do not be conformed to this world, but be transformed by the renewing of your mind."

I didn't realize it was a roadmap for reprogramming.

"Be transformed" — Change is not only possible, it's the goal. You are not meant to stay as you are.

This wasn't just spiritual advice. This was neuroscience written two thousand years ago.

The Bible was telling me: if you want to transform your life, you must first transform your beliefs. And transformed beliefs require a renewed mind.

This verse became the bridge between my faith upbringing and the reprogramming work I would later discover through Dr. Bruce Lipton, Dr. Joe Dispenza, Gregg Braden, and Neville Goddard.

They were all saying the same thing, just in different language: Your mind creates your reality. Change your mind, change your life.

The Awakening: Edgar Cayce, Neville Goddard, and the Inner Kingdom

I was first introduced to meditation when I read a book by Edgar Cayce.

It opened something in me. The idea that I could quiet my mind, go inward, and access wisdom beyond what I'd been taught—this was revolutionary.

When I started meditating, I didn't understand it, I just did it. I didn't even know if I was doing it correctly.

I read "Think and Grow Rich" by Napoleon Hill. I listened to and read books by Neville Goddard. These teachers spoke about the power of imagination, the creative force of thought, and the idea that we are not separate from the divine—we are expressions of it.

And then I started examining the Bible differently.

Not as a rulebook. Not as something to be obeyed without question. But as a text filled with metaphor, wisdom, and teachings that had been interpreted, translated, and edited over centuries.

I began asking: What does it really mean?

"I am the vine, you are the branches." (John 15:5)

When I re-read this verse it blew me away, it all started making sense.

If we are the branches and God is the vine, then we are not separate. We are extensions. We are connected. This isn't about a distant God watching from the clouds—this is about an energy, a source, that flows through us.

"The kingdom of God is within you." (Luke 17:21)

Not in heaven. Not somewhere you go after you die. Within you. Right now. This moment.

If the kingdom is within, then the answers are within. The power is within. The connection is within.

"If they ask you who is this Jesus, tell them 'I AM.'" (Exodus 3:14, John 8:58)

These weren't just religious phrases. They were instructions.

Instructions about how to access the power that exists inside us. Instructions about how to feel as if the prayer is already answered. Instructions about how thought and emotion, when united, create reality.

The Discovery: Gregg Braden and the Lost Books

Then I encountered Gregg Braden.

And everything I had been quietly questioning suddenly had language, context, and evidence.

Gregg Braden spoke about the lost books of the Bible—texts that were removed, edited out, hidden away. Books like the Gospel of Thomas and the Book of Enoch.

The question became: Why were these books removed? What did they contain that someone decided we shouldn't know?

The Gospel of Thomas

The Gospel of Thomas is believed to be the actual words of Jesus as he taught those around him how to use the power of human emotion.

In Verse 48, it says:

This isn't metaphor. This is instruction.

When thought and emotion unite—when you think something and feel it as if it's already true—you access creative power.

And it became true.

The Book of Enoch

The Book of Enoch was removed from the biblical canon, yet it contains profound teachings about ascension, transformation, and the relationship between humanity and the divine.

Enoch was "translated"—which in biblical terms means he ascended. He didn't die. He transformed.

This idea—that transformation is possible, that we are not bound to one state of being, that ascension is available—was too radical for those editing the Bible in the 4th century.

So they removed it.

But the teaching remains: You are not fixed. You can ascend. You can transform.

The Realization: I Had Been Believing in a Bearded Man in the Clouds

For years, I believed in a bearded man sitting in the clouds, watching, judging, deciding who was worthy and who wasn't.

I believed in a devil that caused bad things to happen, a force of evil constantly working against me.

But as I studied, meditated, and questioned, I realized: That belief was keeping me small.

If God is external—somewhere out there, far away, separate from me—then I am powerless. I have to beg. I have to plead. I have to hope that maybe, if I'm good enough, I'll be heard.

But if the kingdom of God is within me, then I am not separate. I am not powerless. I am not at the mercy of an external force.

I am an expression of the divine. And the power to create, heal, and transform is already within me.

This doesn't mean I stopped believing in a higher power. It means I stopped believing that power was distant, judgmental, and separate.

I freed myself from believing in a bearded man in the clouds and a devil causing chaos.

And in that freedom, I found something far more profound: a direct connection to the source. No middleman. No interpreter. No institution required.

The Sensitivity: Why This Runs So Deep

I know this chapter will trigger some people.

Faith runs deep. It's intertwined with identity, family, culture, and survival. For many, questioning faith feels like questioning everything—like the ground beneath them is collapsing.

I understand. Because I felt it too.

When belief becomes identity, questions feel like erasure.

But here's what I've learned: Faith that cannot be questioned is fragile. Faith that allows inquiry becomes personal, expansive, and honest.

I'm not trying to change your mind. I'm simply sharing what I discovered when I dared to ask questions I was told not to ask.

And if you feel anger, fear, or stress reading this—pause and ask yourself: Where is that reaction coming from?

Is it coming from your own direct experience with the divine?

Or is it coming from programming—from what you were told to believe, what you were taught to defend, what you were warned would happen if you questioned?

The Freedom: Spirituality Without the Middleman

I still believe in a higher power. I still pray. I still meditate. I still connect.

But I no longer believe I need permission. I no longer believe I need an institution to tell me how, when, or what to believe.

I have a direct line. And so do you.

You don't have to abandon your faith to examine it. You don't have to reject your tradition to expand it.

But you do have to be willing to ask: Is this belief mine, or was it handed to me?

The Invitation: Examine Your Faith Beliefs

What were you taught to believe about God?

Where did those beliefs come from?

Do those beliefs empower you—or do they keep you dependent, fearful, or small?

What would it feel like to connect directly, without a middleman?

What would change if you believed the kingdom was within you?

I'm not asking you to abandon your faith. I'm asking you to examine whether the faith you hold is truly yours—or whether it's programming.

Because when you examine it, question it, and refine it, something beautiful happens.

You stop performing religion.

And you start living spirituality.

You stop seeking approval from a distant God.

And you start recognizing the divine within.

You stop waiting for permission.

And you start creating.

The bearded man in the clouds never had the power.

You did.

All along.

CHAPTER 16

The Daily Work - Tools and Practices

Reprogramming is not a one-time event. It is a daily practice.

Understanding the science is one thing. Applying it consistently is another. This chapter is about the practical tools and techniques that have transformed my life—not because I did them once, but because I do them daily.

These practices are not theory. They are the work.

Heart-Brain Coherence: The Foundation

I got a lot of information from videos with Gregg Braden, explaining how to breathe and his involvement with the HeartMath Institute. This technique— heart-brain coherence—became the foundation of my daily practice.

What Is Heart-Brain Coherence?

Heart-brain coherence is a state where your heart and brain are synchronized, working in harmony. Research from the HeartMath Institute has shown that when you achieve this state, profound physiological changes occur:

- Stress hormones (cortisol) decrease by 23%

- DHEA (the precursor to all hormones) increases by 100%

- Heart rate variability increases

- Immune responses strengthen

- Longevity enzymes awaken

This isn't just meditation. This is a scientifically measurable state of optimal function.

During coherence, the two branches of the Autonomic Nervous System synchronize with one another, and there is an overall shift toward increased parasympathetic activity (the relaxation response). Different bodily systems synchronize to the rhythm generated by the heart, and there is increased synchronization between the activity of the heart and brain.

In other words: when your heart and brain are coherent, your entire body comes into alignment.

The Quick Coherence Technique

The technique I use is called the Quick Coherence® Technique, developed and refined by the HeartMath Institute. Gregg Braden has taught this technique worldwide, and it has become central to my daily practice.

Here are the steps:

Step 1: Heart Focus

Shift your focus into the area of your heart, and begin to breathe a little more slowly than usual, as if your breath is coming from your heart.

This step alone sends a signal to your body that a shift has taken place—you are no longer engaged in the world around you. You are becoming aware of the world within you.

Step 2: Slow Your Breathing

Allow five to six seconds for your inhale and exhale.

Inhale for a count of four, exhale for a count of six. The longer exhale is key as it activates the parasympathetic nervous system, which encourages a state of calmness.

As you slow your breathing, you are sending a signal to your body that you are safe. It's okay to turn your attention inward.

Step 3: Activate a Positive Feeling

To the best of your ability, feel a genuine sense of caring, appreciation, gratitude, or compassion for anything or anyone. The key to success here is for your feeling to be as sincere and heartfelt as possible. It's the quality of this feeling that fine-tunes and optimizes the coherence between your heart and your brain.

This is where the power lies. Not in thinking positive thoughts—but in feeling positive emotions. Gratitude. Joy. Love. Peace.

It takes about 72 hours (three days) to build these neural networks. The more you do this practice, the stronger this connection becomes in your life.

My Personal Practice

I practice heart-brain coherence every morning and every night.

In the morning, I sit in silence. I shift my focus to my heart. I slow my breathing. And I practice feeling love, joy, gratitude, and peace—not for what I hope will happen, but for what I am choosing to believe is already present.

At night, before I go to bed, I do the same.

This practice doesn't take long. Three to five minutes is enough to create coherence. But the effects can last for hours.

Three minutes of this practice has been shown to increase DHEA levels over 100 percent, lower cortisol levels by 23%, strengthen immune responses, increase heart rate variability, and awaken longevity enzymes.

This is not woo-woo. This is measurable biology.

Theta State: Accessing the Subconscious

In addition to heart-brain coherence, I try to get my mind into theta state.

Theta brainwaves (4-8 Hz) are the state of deep meditation, drowsiness, and the gateway to the subconscious mind. This is the state where reprogramming happens most effectively.

Heart-brain coherence opens the door to a direct link with the subconscious mind.

When you're in theta, your conscious mind steps aside, and your subconscious becomes receptive. This is why affirmations are most powerful when spoken or listened to in this state—either in deep meditation or just before sleep.

High-Frequency Sounds: 432 Hz and Higher

I listen to high-frequency sounds of 432 Hz or higher.

The optimal frequency to harmonize the heart and the brain is 0.1 Hertz, which is also the fundamental frequency of the magnetic fields of the Earth.

I play these frequencies while I meditate, work, or rest. They create an environment that supports coherence, calmness, and receptivity.

Sleep Affirmations: Reprogramming While You Sleep

Why? Because sleep is when the subconscious mind is most open. When your conscious mind is offline, the subconscious absorbs without resistance.

The affirmations I listen to repeat statements like:

- "I am abundant."

- "I am worthy."

- "I am healthy."

- "I am at peace."

- "I am grateful."

Present tense. Stated as fact. Not "I will be" or "I want to be"—but I am.

This is not passive listening. This is active reprogramming.

Dr. Joe Dispenza and Dr. Bruce Lipton both teach that the subconscious mind operates 95% of the time. If you want to change your life, you have to reprogram the subconscious. And sleep is one of the most powerful windows to do that.

Protecting Your Environment: What I Avoid

Reprogramming isn't just about what you expose yourself to—it's also about what you don't expose yourself to.

I avoid:

The News Most news is designed to trigger fear, anger, and stress. Those emotions flood your body with cortisol and adrenaline—the exact opposite of the healing, growth-oriented state I'm cultivating.

Negative Music affects your emotional state. Lyrics that promote violence, scarcity, victimhood, or despair program your subconscious mind. I choose music that uplifts, inspires, or soothes.

Toxic Environments I remove myself from spaces—and people—that reinforce old programming. Not because they're bad, but because their beliefs are contagious. If I'm trying to cultivate abundance and someone around me is constantly speaking scarcity, I have to protect my peace.

Toxic Self-Talk I acknowledge what I am feeling. If it is negative or if it does not serve me, I examine it and replace it.

I don't suppress negative emotions. I don't pretend they don't exist. But I also don't allow them to run unchecked.

When a negative thought arises, I pause. I ask:

- Where did this come from?

- Is this true?

- Does this serve who I am becoming?

And then I replace it.

Service: Love Your Neighbor as Yourself

I volunteer my time. My choice is the food bank, but the specific place doesn't matter as much as the act itself.

Service is one of the most powerful ways to shift out of scarcity and into abundance. When you give, you reinforce the belief that there is enough. That you have enough. That you are enough.

When I look at someone, I try to remember that. Not as a moral obligation, but as a practice of coherence. When I see others with compassion, I am also seeing myself with compassion.

The Daily Rhythm: Morning and Night

Here is my daily rhythm:

Morning:

1. Meditation (5-10 minutes)

- Heart-brain coherence

- Feeling gratitude, joy, love, peace

2. Affirmations (spoken aloud or listened to)

- "I am" statements in present tense

3. 432 Hz frequency sounds (playing in the background as I start my day)

Throughout the Day:

- Conscious breathing when I feel stress

- Pausing to return to heart-brain coherence

- Protecting my environment (avoiding negativity)

- Service and compassion toward others

Night:

1. Meditation (5-10 minutes)

- Heart-brain coherence

- Reviewing the day with gratitude

2. Sleep affirmations (8+ hours)

- Playing throughout the night while I sleep

The Science: Why This Works

Gregg Braden healed a tumor in two weeks using heart-brain coherence.

Gregg was diagnosed with a growth on his bladder. For two weeks, he practiced communicating with his body and placed himself in heart-brain coherence. He went into surgery and woke up to his physician asking him why he was in the hospital if nothing was wrong with him. Gregg was able to heal his bladder tumor through brain-heart coherence in the time span of two weeks.

This isn't a miracle. It's biology responding to coherence.

With our mind, we reach into quantum possibilities. We imagine our healing, we imagine peace, we imagine abundance. And with our heart, we give that possibility life. We breathe life into the image of our mind through the feeling in our heart and make it real in our world.

The mind imagines. The heart feels. Together, they create.

This is not wishful thinking. This is quantum biology.

The Invitation: Start Small, Stay Consistent

You don't have to do everything I do.

Start with one practice. Just one.

Try three minutes of heart-brain coherence in the morning. Or listen to sleep affirmations tonight. Or avoid the news for one week and notice how you feel.

The key is consistency.

It takes about 72 hours to build these neural networks. The more you practice, the stronger the connection becomes.

Reprogramming is not dramatic. It's cumulative.

Small, consistent actions compound into transformation.

Reflection Questions

Which of these practices resonates most with you?

What is one tool you can implement today?

What environments or influences do you need to protect yourself from?

How would your life change if you practiced heart-brain coherence daily?

The work is simple. But simple doesn't mean easy.

It requires commitment. Consistency. And the willingness to choose your inner state over external chaos.

But the reward is freedom.

Freedom from fear. Freedom from reactivity. Freedom from inherited programming.

And the life you create from that freedom is worth every moment of practice.

CHAPTER 17

When Old Beliefs Return - Maintenance and Mastery

Reprogramming is not a destination. It is a journey.

And like any journey, there are days when you move forward with ease—and days when you find yourself back where you started, wondering if anything has changed at all.

This has been an ongoing process and practice for me. I continue to learn and grow. I have had setbacks. And when I do, I simply return to what I know has worked for me.

This chapter is about what happens after the breakthrough—when the old beliefs return, when doubt creeps back in, when the voice you thought you silenced starts speaking again.

Because it will happen. And when it does, you need to know: that doesn't mean you've failed.

It means you're human.

The Truth About Reprogramming: It's Not Linear

I used to think that once I reprogrammed a belief, it was gone forever. That once I replaced the old self-talk with new self-talk, the transformation was permanent.

But that's not how it works.

Old beliefs don't disappear. They quiet down. They step back. But they don't vanish.

They are still there—in the neural pathways carved by years of repetition, in the emotional memory stored in your body, in the environments and relationships that reinforced them.

And under stress, under pressure, under fear—they resurface.

This doesn't mean the work didn't matter. It means the work is ongoing.

When Old Beliefs Return: My Experience

Even now, after all the work I've done, old beliefs still show up.

The belief that I'm not safe—that something bad is about to happen—still surfaces when I'm stressed.

The belief that I have to work twice as hard to get half as much—that still whispers when I see others succeed with what looks like ease.

The belief that asking for help is weakness—that still shows up when I'm struggling and my first instinct is to handle it alone.

These beliefs don't control me the way they used to. But they're still there.

And when they return, I have a choice:

I can spiral. I can believe the old story. I can let the voice take over and convince me that nothing has changed.

Or I can pause. I can recognize the voice. I can acknowledge it without obeying it.

And I can return to what I know works.

The Pattern: How Old Beliefs Resurface

Old beliefs tend to return in predictable patterns:

1. During Stress or Crisis

When your nervous system is activated—when you're under pressure, facing a deadline, dealing with conflict—your brain defaults to the oldest, most familiar programming.

This is survival mode. And in survival mode, the subconscious takes over.

The beliefs you've been reprogramming are stored in the conscious mind and the new neural pathways you've been building. But under stress, the brain reaches for what's fastest and most automatic—the old pathways.

2. In Familiar Environments

If you return to an environment where the old belief was formed—whether that's a family gathering, an old job, or even just a specific location—the belief can be triggered.

Environments hold emotional memory. Your body remembers how it felt in that space, what was expected of you, what was safe and what wasn't.

This is why going home for the holidays can feel like stepping back in time. The environment activates the old programming, even if you've done years of work to change it.

3. Around People Who Reinforce the Old Belief

Certain people carry the voice of your old programming.

Maybe it's a parent who still treats you like a child. A friend who still sees you as you were, not as you're becoming. A colleague who reinforces scarcity thinking.

You can be in the middle of transformation—and one conversation with the wrong person can make you question everything.

This doesn't mean those people are bad. It means their beliefs are contagious. And if you're not careful, you'll absorb them again.

4. After Success

This one surprised me.

I thought old beliefs would return during failure—when things went wrong, when I made mistakes, when I didn't get the result I wanted.

But they also return after success.

Success can trigger the belief that you're not supposed to have it. That it's too good to be true. That the universe is about to correct the imbalance.

What to Do When Old Beliefs Return

When the old belief resurfaces, here's what I do:

Step 1: Recognize It

The first step is awareness. Notice when the old voice is speaking.

Don't judge it. Don't shame yourself for it. Just notice it.

Step 2: Acknowledge It Without Obeying It

You can acknowledge a thought without believing it.

This is the difference between reaction and response.

Reaction is automatic. Response is conscious.

When you acknowledge the belief without obeying it, you're responding instead of reacting. You're creating space between the trigger and your action.

Step 3: Return to the Practice

This is where the daily work pays off.

When the old belief returns, I don't try to fight it or force it away. I return to the practices I know work:

- Heart-brain coherence to calm my nervous system

- Meditation to reconnect with the present moment

- Affirmations to reinforce the new belief

- Gratitude to shift from fear to trust

- Examining the thought to trace it back to its source

The tools don't stop working just because the belief returned. The belief returned because stress, environment, or proximity triggered the old programming.

But the new programming is still there. You just have to activate it again.

Step 4: Be Compassionate With Yourself

This is not perfection. It is a journey.

You are not failing when old beliefs return. You are human.

The goal is not to eliminate all doubt, all fear, all old programming forever. The goal is to recognize it faster, question it sooner, and choose differently more often.

Progress is not perfection. Progress is awareness.

The Tire Shop Moment: A Recent Example

I told you earlier about the tire shop incident—when I accused the dealership of putting nails in my tire.

That was an old belief resurfacing. The automatic distrust. The assumption that I was being scammed. The inherited programming from a community that has been lied to for generations.

I didn't catch it in the moment. The belief spoke before I could question it.

But I caught it afterward. I examined it. I traced it back to its source. I asked whether it served me.

And I chose not to reinforce it.

That's the work. Not perfection—but awareness and course correction.

The Setbacks: What I've Learned

I've had setbacks. Times when I reverted to old patterns. Times when I doubted everything I had learned. Times when I wondered if any of this reprogramming work actually mattered.

Here's what I've learned from those setbacks:

1. Setbacks Are Not Failures—They're Feedback

When you slip back into an old belief, it's not proof that the work didn't matter. It's feedback showing you where the old programming is still strong—and where you need to reinforce the new programming.

2. The New Programming Gets Stronger Each Time You Return to It

Every time you recognize an old belief and choose the new one instead, you strengthen the new neural pathway.

It's like a muscle. The more you use it, the stronger it gets.

The first time you catch yourself and choose differently, it's hard. The tenth time, it's easier. The hundredth time, it's automatic.

3. You Don't Have to Start Over—You Just Return

When old beliefs resurface, you don't lose all your progress. You don't go back to square one.

You just return to the practice.

You don't have to rebuild from scratch. You just have to remember what works and do it again.

4. The Journey Never Ends—And That's Okay

There is no finish line where all old beliefs are gone and all new beliefs are permanent.

This is lifelong work. Lifelong practice. Lifelong growth.

And that's not a burden. That's freedom.

Because it means you're never stuck. You're always evolving. You're always becoming.

The Practice of Maintenance

Maintenance is not about perfection. It's about consistency.

Here's what maintenance looks like for me:

Daily:

- Morning and evening meditation (even if it's just 3 minutes)

- Heart-brain coherence when I feel stress

- Sleep affirmations playing throughout the night

- Checking my thoughts and replacing what doesn't serve me

Weekly:

- Reviewing my affirmations and updating them as I grow

- Noticing patterns—when do old beliefs resurface? What triggers them?

- Protecting my environment—saying no to toxic spaces, people, or content

Monthly:

- Reflecting on progress—not perfection, but awareness

- Asking: What belief is still showing up? What needs more attention?

- Celebrating wins—even small ones

Ongoing:

- Returning to the work when setbacks happen

- Being compassionate with myself

- Remembering that this is a journey, not a destination

Mastery Is Not Perfection—It's Recognition

Mastery doesn't mean you never have old beliefs return. Mastery means you recognize them faster.

A beginner might spiral for days before realizing they're stuck in old programming.

Someone with practice might catch it after a few hours.

Someone with mastery catches it in the moment—or even before it fully takes hold.

Mastery is not the absence of old beliefs. Mastery is the ability to recognize them, acknowledge them, and choose differently.

And that ability gets stronger the more you practice.

The Invitation: Keep Going

It came back because that's what old beliefs do. They don't disappear. They quiet down. And under the right conditions, they speak again.

But here's what matters:

You now have tools you didn't have before. You now have awareness you didn't have before. You now have choice you didn't have before.

The belief may return. But you don't have to obey it.

And every time you choose the new belief over the old one, you get stronger.

Every time you return to the practice, the neural pathway deepens.

Every time you catch yourself and course-correct, you prove to yourself that transformation is possible.

This is not perfection. It is a journey.

And the journey is worth it.

Reflection Questions

What old belief has resurfaced for you recently?

What triggered it—stress, environment, a person, success?

How did you respond? Did you recognize it, or did it take over?

What practice can you return to when old beliefs resurface?

How can you be more compassionate with yourself during setbacks?

The work is not about eliminating all old programming. The work is about recognizing it, questioning it, and choosing differently.

And you're already doing that.

You're already on the path.

Keep going.

85

CONCLUSION

The Invitation

This book began with a simple truth: some of the strongest beliefs in my life were never questioned.

They were handed down, absorbed, internalized—and for years, I lived inside them without knowing I had a choice.

If you've made it this far, you likely see yourself in these pages. You've recognized the voice that isn't yours. You've felt the weight of beliefs you never chose. You've sensed that something is off, even if you couldn't name it.

That sensing—that discomfort, that doubt, that quiet knowing—is not a problem.

It is an invitation.

An invitation to examine what you've been taught. An invitation to question what you've accepted as truth. An invitation to reclaim authority over your own mind.

This work is not easy. It requires courage to ask, "Who said so?" It takes strength to face the possibility that people you love, institutions you trusted, and beliefs you held sacred may have been incomplete, outdated, or simply wrong for you.

But the alternative—living a life governed by programming you never consented to—is far more costly.

Here is what I want you to know:

You are not broken for questioning. You are not disloyal for seeking truth. You are not weak for wanting something different.

You are waking up.

And waking up is the beginning of freedom.

The beliefs you inherited were formed in a specific context, for a specific time, often with the best intentions. But you are not required to carry them forever. You have permission to examine them. To keep what serves you. To release what doesn't. To replace what limits you with what expands you.

This is not about rejecting your past. It is about refusing to let your past dictate your future.

The work of reprogramming is ongoing. Old beliefs will resurface. Doubt will whisper. Fear will try to pull you back to what's familiar. But now you have tools. You have awareness. You have choice.

When the voice in your head says, "This is just how it is," you can ask: Is it? Or is this just what I was taught to believe?

When fear tells you to stay small, you can ask: Whose fear is this? And does it still serve me?

When guilt says you're being selfish for choosing yourself, you can ask: Who benefits from me believing that?

These questions are not rebellion. They are responsibility.

You are not required to live according to someone else's programming. You are not obligated to accept inherited limitations as your destiny. You are not bound by beliefs that were true for others but not true for you.

You have the power to rewrite the code.

Not through wishful thinking, but through deliberate practice. Through examination, questioning, and conscious choice. Through alignment of belief, thought, and action.

The abundant life—the conscious life, the free life—is not waiting for permission. It is waiting for you to claim it.

So I leave you with this:

What belief are you ready to question? What voice are you ready to silence? What truth are you ready to speak?

The work begins with one question. One examination. One choice.

And that choice changes everything.

Welcome to the other side of questioning.

Welcome to the life you were always meant to live—the one you get to consciously create.

The programming is not permanent.

The choice is yours.

And you are more powerful than you have been taught to believe.

ABOUT THE AUTHOR

Robin DeFleice is a transformational author, real estate professional, and advocate for conscious living who discovered the power of reprogramming beliefs after decades of living according to someone else's rules.

Raised in a family and culture that valued obedience over questioning, she spent years living by beliefs she never consciously chose—about money, health, relationships, identity, and faith. As a case manager, she witnessed firsthand how people can remain trapped in systems that claim to help, yet often reinforce cycles of dependency and limitation.

Everything changed when she began to question.

At an age when many people settle into "the way things are," Robin chose reinvention. At 62, she earned her associate degree. Just 18 months later, she completed her bachelor's degree. At 66, she purchased her first home—proving that growth and new beginnings are not limited by age.

Her journey from inherited programming to conscious choice led her to study the work of Dr. Bruce Lipton, Dr. Joe Dispenza, Gregg Braden, Dr. Caroline Leaf, Neville Goddard, and Joyce Meyer. She discovered that ancient biblical wisdom and modern neuroscience often point to the same truth: transformation happens through the renewing of the mind.

Through daily practices of meditation, affirmations, gratitude, and intentional reprogramming, she reversed her Type 2 diabetes, released limiting identities, and created a life rooted in abundance, peace, and purpose.

Today, she helps others recognize the beliefs they never chose and reclaim authority over their own minds. She volunteers regularly at a local food bank and lives by the principle that questioning is not rebellion—it is awakening.

Robin DeFleice is also the author of:

- It's Never Too Late: Reinventing Yourself After 60

- The Home Buyer Edge: A Smart Home Buying Guide for Women Over 40

She lives in Cleveland, Ohio, where she continues to learn, grow, and challenge the beliefs that no longer serve her—one conscious choice at a time.

Connect with the Author

Website: robindefleice.com

Email: Defleicerobin@yahoo.com

Social media: youtube.com/@RobinDeFleice

APPENDIX A

Belief Inventory Worksheet

Use this worksheet to identify and examine the beliefs that may be limiting you. Be honest. Write without judgment.

Part 1: Identifying Inherited Beliefs

About Money:

- What were you told about money growing up?

- What did you observe about how your family handled money?

- Complete this sentence: "Money is ________________"

- Complete this sentence: "Rich people are ________________"

- What do you believe is possible for you financially?

About Health:

- What were you taught about your body?

- What beliefs do you hold about illness, aging, or healing?

- Do you trust your body's signals, or do you override them?

- Complete this sentence: "My body is ________________"

- What health outcomes do you believe are inevitable?

About Relationships:

- What were you taught about love, marriage, or partnership?

- Complete this sentence: "All men are ________________"

- Complete this sentence: "All women are ________________"

- What do you believe you must do to be accepted by others?

- What relationships are you staying in out of fear rather than choice?

About Your Identity:

- How do you usually introduce yourself?

- What labels do you use to describe yourself?

- Which of these labels were given to you vs. chosen by you?

- Complete this sentence: "I'm the kind of person who __________________"

- Complete this sentence: "I'm not the kind of person who __________________"

About Faith/Spirituality:

- What were you taught about God, the divine, or spirituality?

- What questions have you been afraid to ask?

- What beliefs bring you peace vs. what beliefs create fear?

- Do your spiritual beliefs empower you or make you feel small?

Part 2: Tracing the Source

For each limiting belief you identified above, ask:

1. Where did this belief come from?

- Whose voice does it sound like?

- When did I first learn this?

2. What evidence do I have that this belief is true?

- Is it based on my direct experience?

- Or is it based on what I was told?

3. Who benefits from me believing this?

- Does this belief serve me?

- Or does it serve a system, institution, or person?

4. What would be possible if I didn't believe this?

- How would my life be different?

- What would I attempt that I'm not attempting now?

Part 3: Choosing New Beliefs

For each limiting belief, create a replacement:

Old Belief: ____________________________________

New Belief: _______________________________________

Evidence for New Belief: _______________________________________

Action I Will Take Based on New Belief: _______________________________________

APPENDIX B

Daily Reprogramming Checklist

Use this checklist to track your daily practices. Consistency is key.

Morning Practice (5-15 minutes)

☐ Heart-Brain Coherence (3-5 minutes)

- Focus on heart area

- Slow breathing (4-second inhale, 6-second exhale)

- Feel gratitude, joy, love, or peace

☐ Spoken Affirmations

- Read or speak your "I Am" statements

- Say them with feeling, not just words

- Present tense, as if already true

☐ Set Intention for the Day

- What belief am I practicing today?

- What old pattern am I choosing not to repeat?

Throughout the Day

☐ Catch Negative Self-Talk

- When you notice a limiting thought, pause

- Ask: Where did this come from? Is it true?

- Replace it with your new belief

☐ Return to Coherence When Stressed

- Three conscious breaths focused on your heart

- Shift from fear to gratitude

☐ Protect Your Environment

- Avoid negative news/media

- Distance from toxic conversations

- Choose uplifting content

Evening Practice (5-15 minutes)

☐ Meditation/Heart-Brain Coherence

- Review the day with gratitude

- Release what didn't serve you

- Prepare your mind for sleep

☐ Sleep Affirmations (8+ hours)

- Play "I Am" affirmations throughout the night

- Allow subconscious reprogramming while you sleep

☐ 432 Hz or Higher Frequency Sounds (optional)

- Play healing frequencies as you fall asleep

Weekly Review

☐ What old belief surfaced this week?

☐ How did I respond to it?

☐ What practice helped me most?

☐ What needs more attention?

APPENDIX C

Recommended Reading & Resources

Books on Reprogramming & Belief

The Biology of Belief by Dr. Bruce Lipton

- Epigenetics and how beliefs affect your biology

Breaking the Habit of Being Yourself by Dr. Joe Dispenza

- Neuroscience of changing your mind and your life

Becoming Supernatural by Dr. Joe Dispenza

- Advanced techniques for transformation

The Power of Your Subconscious Mind by Joseph Murphy

- Classic text on subconscious reprogramming

Think and Grow Rich by Napoleon Hill

- Mindset and wealth-building principles

Feeling Is the Secret by Neville Goddard

- The power of feeling your desires as already fulfilled

The Power of Awareness by Neville Goddard

- Imagination and consciousness create reality

Battlefield of the Mind by Joyce Meyer

- Biblical approach to renewing your mind

Books on Faith & Spirituality

The Isaiah Effect by Gregg Braden

- Ancient wisdom and quantum science

The Divine Matrix by Gregg Braden

- Bridging time, space, miracles, and belief

The God Code by Gregg Braden

- DNA and the language of God

The Gospel of Thomas (Translation by Elaine Pagels or Marvin Meyer)

-   Lost teachings of Jesus

The Book of Enoch (Various translations available)

-   Ancient text removed from biblical canon

Online Resources

HeartMath Institute (www.heartmath.org)

-   Research on heart-brain coherence

-   Free tools and techniques

Dr. Joe Dispenza's Website (drjoedispenza.com)

-   Meditations, courses, and workshops

Gregg Braden's Website (greggbraden.com)

-   Videos, courses, and teachings

Dr. Bruce Lipton's Website (brucelipton.com)

-   Research and educational materials

Audio/Video Resources

YouTube Channels:

-   Gregg Braden (teachings on heart-brain coherence, lost gospels)

-   Dr. Joe Dispenza (guided meditations)

-   Joyce Meyer Ministries (biblical teaching on renewing the mind)

-   Neville Goddard Lectures (audio recordings)

Sleep Affirmations:

-   Search YouTube for "I Am affirmations 8 hours"

-   Search for "432 Hz sleep meditation"

-   Look for channels that offer long-form (8-12 hour) affirmations

Frequency Sounds:

-   432 Hz (natural frequency, harmony)

-   528 Hz (transformation and miracles)

- 741 Hz (awakening intuition)

- 963 Hz (connection to divine)

APPENDIX D

Journal Prompts by Chapter

Use these prompts to deepen your understanding and integration of each chapter's teachings.

Chapter 2: The Beliefs I Never Chose

- What belief did you accept as truth without questioning?

- What was the "cap on the jar" in your life?

- When did you first realize you had a choice?

Chapter 3: Who Taught Me What to Believe

- Who were your primary teachers of belief? (family, church, school, media)

- What beliefs did you absorb that you never consciously chose?

- Which authority figures did you stop questioning—and why?

Chapter 4: When Belief Becomes the Voice in Your Head

- What does your inner voice sound like?

- Whose voice is it really? (mother, father, teacher, culture)

- What does your self-talk say about money? Health? Relationships? Your worth?

Chapter 5: Tracing the Voice

- Write down three negative thoughts you've had this week

- For each one, ask: Where did this come from? Whose voice is this?

- What would a compassionate, truthful reframe sound like?

Chapter 6: When Systems Are Mistaken for Healers

- What system have you trusted without questioning? (healthcare, education, finance, religion)

- When did you surrender your authority to an institution?

- What would it look like to reclaim responsibility without rejecting support?

Chapter 7: The Cost of Unquestioned Belief

- What has unquestioned belief cost you? (health, relationships, opportunities, peace)

- What belief are you still "applying butter to the burn" with?

- What price are you paying to stay loyal to someone else's truth?

Chapter 8: The Search for Truth

- What belief did you question that caused doubt and confusion?

- What did you discover when you started investigating?

- What programming are you ready to rewrite?

Chapter 9: The Work of Reprogramming

- What is your current daily practice?

- What environments or people reinforce your old programming?

- What would it look like to protect your peace more intentionally?

Chapter 10: Acting As If

- What decision have you been afraid to make?

- What would "acting as if" look like in your life right now?

- What affirmation can you write in present tense that scares you—but also excites you?

Chapter 11: Money - From Scarcity to Abundance

- What were you told about money growing up?

- What scarcity beliefs are you still operating from?

- What would abundance thinking look like for you?

Chapter 12: Health - From Compliance to Body Wisdom

- What beliefs do you hold about your body?

- When do you override your body's signals?

- What would it mean to trust your body instead of controlling it?

Chapter 13: Relationships - From Herd Mentality to Self-Approval

APPENDIX E

Sample Affirmations by Category

Use these as templates. Customize them to fit your specific beliefs and goals. Always use present tense "I Am" statements.

Money & Abundance

- I am financially abundant.

- Money flows to me easily and effortlessly.

- I am worthy of wealth.

- I create value and I am compensated generously.

- I am grateful for the abundance in my life.

- My income increases consistently.

- I make wise financial decisions.

- I am the top [your profession] in [your area].

Health & Body

- I am healthy and vibrant.

- My body knows how to heal.

- I trust my body's wisdom.

- I am strong, energized, and alive.

- Every cell in my body functions perfectly.

- I nourish my body with love and care.

- I am grateful for my body's strength.

- Health is my natural state.

Relationships & Connection

- I am surrounded by loving, supportive people.

- I attract authentic relationships.

- I am worthy of love exactly as I am.

- I give and receive love freely.

- My boundaries are respected.

- I am connected to a community that celebrates me.

- I choose relationships that honor my growth.

Identity & Self-Worth

- I am enough, exactly as I am.

- I am powerful beyond measure.

- I am worthy of all good things.

- I trust myself completely.

- I honor my voice and my truth.

- I am becoming the highest version of myself.

- I am free to be who I truly am.

Faith & Spirituality

- I am connected to the divine within me.

- The kingdom of God is within me.

- I am an expression of infinite love.

- I trust the guidance of my higher self.

- I am aligned with my purpose.

- I walk in faith, not fear.

- I am transforming through the renewing of my mind.

Peace & Presence

- I am at peace.

- I am calm and centered.

- I trust the timing of my life.

- I release what no longer serves me.

- I am present in this moment.

- I choose peace over worry.

- I am grateful for this day.

A Final Word

These appendices are tools—not rules.

Use what serves you. Adapt what needs adapting. Release what doesn't resonate.

The work of reprogramming is deeply personal. What works for one person may not work for another. Trust your own discernment.

But whatever you do—be consistent.

Transformation is not dramatic. It is cumulative.

Small, daily actions compound into profound change.

You don't have to do everything. You just have to do something.

And then do it again tomorrow.

The beliefs you never chose are not permanent.

The programming can be rewritten.

And the life you were told wasn't possible?

It's waiting for you on the other side of questioning.

Keep going.